LISTENING
BEHAVIOR

Larry L. Barker
Florida State University

LISTENING BEHAVIOR

Prentice-Hall, Inc.
Englewood Cliffs, N.J.

Library of Congress Catalog Card Number: 78-143587

Printed in the United States of America

13-537126-0

Current Printing (last digit):

10 9 8 7 6 5 4 3 2 1

PRENTICE-HALL INTERNATIONAL, INC., London
PRENTICE-HALL OF AUSTRALIA, PTY. LTD., Sydney
PRENTICE-HALL OF CANADA, LTD., Toronto
PRENTICE-HALL OF INDIA PRIVATE LIMITED, New Delhi
PRENTICE-HALL OF JAPAN, INC., Tokyo

CONTENTS

Chapter 6

LISTENING TO
BIASED COMMUNICATION   85

Chapter 7

Kathy J. Wahlers

LISTENER FEEDBACK
AND RESPONSE   106

PREFACE

This book is intended to supplement basic texts in such areas as speech communication, business, guidance and counseling, and education. It also may serve as a primary text in courses focusing directly on the listening process. The text is written primarily for college undergraduates—not listening theorists or communication theorists. Although much of the content is based on descriptive and experimental research in the area of listening, an attempt has been made to minimize the use of professional "jargon" and to discuss listening principles in a straightforward non-technical manner.

Several motivating forces stimulated the writing of this text. Among them were beliefs that (1) most of us take the listening process for granted; (2) most of us are less effective listeners than we could be; and (3) the failure to listen probably creates more interpersonal (and, perhaps, international) problems than any other aspect of human behavior. Although no book can solve all of man's problems, it is hoped that this text will provide a foundation for the solution of one of man's deficiencies—ineffective listening.

The reader will note a consistent emphasis on objectives throughout the text. This is due to a firm belief that the specification of objectives can help one comprehend textual material more efficiently and provide advance "cues" to the important elements of content in each chapter. The objectives also should prove useful for teachers, since objectives serve as bases for examination questions. The inclusion of complete summaries at the end of chapters also reflects a conviction that learning is most effective when important information is repeated several times in slightly different forms. The summaries also can serve as "built-in" reviews for students when preparing for tests over the chapters. *Content* (and at times *Action*) objectives are specified at the beginning of each chapter. However, there are several *general* objectives which may be specified for the entire text. These are:

(1) To provide the reader with an appreciation for listening as a vital element in the communication process.

(2) To provide the reader with a basic understanding of listening behavior and the listening process.

(3) To "sensitize" the reader to his own listening behavior.

(4) To help the reader improve his listening proficiencies in a variety of listening settings.

(5) To provide the reader with criteria with which to evaluate his own listening behavior.

(6) To stimulate readers to actively attempt to help their friends, relatives and acquaintances improve their listening behaviors.

I gratefully acknowledge the influence of countless listening scholars whose ideas and thoughts pervade the entire text. Special debts of gratitude must be expressed to Ralph Nichols, Leonard Stevens, Thomas Lewis, Dominick Barbara, Sam Duker, and Charles Petrie, whose writings and research on listening provided the bases for much of the content of this volume. I also am grateful for the willing assistance of several friends and colleagues who contributed, at various stages, to the ideas, format, and/or editing of this manuscript. These include Bob Kibler, John Pacilio, Kathy Wahlers, Kenny Scruggs, Mary Dollard and Arthur Rittenberg. A special "thank you" is extended to my wife, Jeanne, who transcribed and typed the entire manuscript, and managed to keep her pleasant disposition throughout it all.

LISTENING QUIZ

Before beginning to read this text, answer, to the best of your ability, the following eleven true-false questions regarding the listening process. After you have completed the quiz, turn the page to check your answers.

T_____ F_____ 1. Listening is largely a matter of intelligence.

T_____ F_____ 2. Speaking is a more important part of the communication process than listening.

T_____ F_____ 3. Listening requires little energy, it is "easy."

T_____ F_____ 4. Listening is an automatic, involuntary reflex.

T_____ F_____ 5. Speakers can command listening to occur within an audience.

T_____ F_____ 6. Hearing ability significantly determines listening ability.

T_____ F_____ 7. The speaker is totally responsible for the success of communication.

T_____ F_____ 8. People listen everyday. This daily practice eliminates the need for listening training.

T_____ F_____ 9. Competence in listening develops naturally.

T_____ F_____ 10. When you learned to read, you simultaneously learned to listen.

T_____ F_____ 11. Listening is only a matter of understanding the words of the speaker.

Turn the page for answers!

ANSWERS TO
LISTENING QUIZ

All of the statements on the previous page were false. If you marked one or more of them true, this text should be extremely valuable in helping you gain a deeper understanding as to the listening process, and particularly, into the role of the active listener in the communication process. If you marked all of the statements false, congratulations! You already are aware of some basic principles concerning listening which many people do not realize. The text should reinforce your ideas regarding listening and help you channel your listening energy more effectively by providing some guidelines for isolating listening problems and improving your listening skills.

Theodore Clevenger, Jr.*

LISTENING
BEHAVIOR:
PREVIEW AND
PERSPECTIVE

The following passage previews the concept of listening behavior and establishes a perspective for this text. The primary purpose of the passage is to outline some variables which affect listening behavior. In addition, it serves to identify and emphasize some important characteristics of effective listeners.

. . . .

Any analysis of individual auditors must begin with the recognition that listening is behavior. It is an ancient and obvious truism—but one often overlooked—that listening is not a passive activity. Even the most relaxed and effortless sort of listening, such as one might give in response to music, light drama, or a humorous after-dinner talk, involves doing something. In certain instances, superficial analysis may give the impression that the listener, though undergoing changes and hence "active" in that sense of the word, is in reality a "passive" instrument in the hands of a skilled communicator who activates desired responses in the listener by administering the correct sequence of stimuli. However, more detailed examination reveals a very different picture, one in which the listener plays a much more active role in determining both the nature and the outcome of the communicative encounter. The auditor is involved in a con-

* An excerpt from Theodore Clevenger, Jr. *Audience analysis.* Indianapolis, Indiana: Bobbs-Merrill, Inc., 1966. Pages 7-9, reprinted by permission.

tinuous sequence of behavior, only some of which is under the apparent control of the speaker. Much of the presumed audience control of skillful public speakers resides not so much in their ability to manipulate audiences as in their adroitness at fitting their speeches to ongoing behavioral patterns and tendencies in the audience. Viewed from this standpoint, the behavior of the audience may have as great an influence upon the speaker as his behavior has upon the audience. But regardless of the net balance of influence, it is clear that listening, like all other human activity, consists of the behavior of individuals.

Because listening is behavior, it is governed by the same principles that govern all other behavior. The total constellation of factors influencing such complex behaviors as often arise in the speaking-listening situation is not completely understood, but it is clear that several levels and types of learning are involved. Although the point has not been fully proved, it is a good working hypothesis that whatever people do in any situation (including the listening situation) will be consistent with what they have learned to do both in that situation and in other situations that they think to be relevant to it. Furthermore, until we have convincing evidence to the contrary, it seems sensible to presume that the individual does not change basically when cast in the role of auditor; that is, what he does as a listener grows out of the same habits, values, beliefs, and motives that serve as references for his behavior in other settings.

To suggest that the same factors that control an individual's listening behavior also control his other behaviors is to imply that he brings to the listening situation all of his previous experience. In other words, how an individual responds on a given occasion is a product of the stimuli of the moment as interpreted in the light of his life history. Of course, not every previous experience will be relevant to any given moment's behavior; but even the question of which experiences are relevant is determined by perceptions, habits, values, and so forth, which are themselves products of experience, and hence individual. The point is that the auditor brings much more than some imaginary and universal "listening faculty" to the communicative setting; he enters the setting as an individual whole and entire, bringing the residue of his whole life's experience with him.

To say that the individual comes to the listening situation with all of his prior experience at hand is not to imply that he will respond uniformly to the same message in every situation. Quite the reverse is true, for part of his experience will have taught him to discriminate among a very great variety of different contexts. An isolated stimulus occurring in one context may elicit from him a very different response from that elicited by the same stimulus occurring in a different context. Among all his responses, these rules of context play a particularly important role, and often account for apparent inconsistencies in behavior. Most people are able to distinguish among many different situations in which they are receivers of communications. In each of these situations a slightly different set of perceptions and response tendencies may be called forth. To some stimuli the individual will respond uniformly in all of these discriminably different contexts; but other stimuli will lead to responses that differ markedly from one context to another. Again it is important to emphasize that "context" is here determined by the individual; two sets of circumstances that represent essentially identical contexts for one person may represent quite different contexts for another.

Any attempt to understand auditors must be guided by the recognition that listening is behavior; that as behavior it is controlled by the same principles that govern other types of behavior; that the auditor interprets an incoming message within the framework of his prior experience; and that this interpretation will be carried out under whatever rules of context the individual auditor has learned to apply in communication situations.

.   .   .   .

LISTENING BEHAVIOR

INTRODUCTION

Content Objectives for Chapter 1

After completing this chapter, you should be able to:

(1) Describe, orally or in writing, the differences between a message receiver and a listener.

(2) List approximate percentages of time adults spend listening, reading, writing, and speaking during their waking day.

(3) Describe, orally or in writing, the relative amount of time students spend listening in the classroom; contrast this with the amount of time many teachers think students spend listening in the classroom.

(4) List at least five rewards for active listening in a serious setting.

(5) List at least five rewards for active listening in a social setting.

(6) Define and differentiate between:

    (a) serious and social listening settings
    (b) active and passive listening
    (c) critical and discriminative listening

(7) Define and differentiate among four different levels of classroom listening.

Visualize, if you will, the following communication situations: (1) You peer through an open door into a history classroom where the professor is delivering his lecture in an extremely entertaining and animated fashion. As you glance around the room you note that there are no students present—just the professor giving his lecture. (2) There is an open-air rally on campus concerning elections for student body president. A candidate is standing on the steps of the administration building eloquently outlining his campaign platform to rows and rows of empty chairs. (3) You walk into a radio station and see one of the latest popular records revolving on a turntable inside the studio. However, upon looking around, you find that the station's transmitter is not turned on.

It does not take a very critical observer to note that the basic element missing in each of these communication situations is an audience or receiver of the respective messages. Now, visualize these same three communication situations again and assume there are people present in addition to the message originators. The classroom is filled with students, the campus rally attracts hundreds of eager college students, and the radio station transmitter is operating, allowing the audience to tune in their radios and hear music. At this point, can we assume that successful communication will necessarily occur? Emphatically, "No!" because communication involves more than the mere physical presence of a message originator (speaker) and a receiver—it involves active participation and mutual concern by both the speaker and the receiver-responder (listener). In the three examples above, if members of the audience are actively attempting to absorb and understand the message being transmitted, then listening and communication will take place. If, on the other hand, audience members are not actively involved in the listening process, communication failure or breakdown will occur in every instance.

In succeeding chapters the listening process will be described and some desirable and undesirable characteristics of listeners will be reviewed. However, as the above illustrations point out, the mere presence of a message receiver does not guarantee that communication will take place—the listener must be "tuned in" to the speaker before communication can be successful. The difference between merely receiving an oral message and listening actively is similar to the difference between scanning a textbook and reading it for comprehension and retention. When you scan written material you cannot fully appreciate or understand many of the author's ideas and subtle distinctions. On the other hand, when you read a text intently, as you might the night before an important examination, you are more likely to interpret correctly—and, perhaps, better appreciate—the message the author intended to convey. In oral communication settings there must be involved * listeners attempting to internalize and evaluate the message in order for a speaker to achieve his communication objective.

How Much Time Do You Spend Listening?

Did you ever stop to think how much time you spend listening during the average day? You probably would be surprised at the amount. Several studies have attempted to ascertain the amount of time people in different occupations spend listening. The earliest study, and perhaps the most thoroughly executed, was by Rankin in 1929. He asked adults in a variety of occupations to keep a record, at fifteen-minute intervals during their waking day, of the approximate amount of time they spent in four different types of verbal communication: reading, writing, listening, and speaking. Rankin's subjects reported that about 70 percent of their waking day was spent in one or more of the four kinds of communication. When the relative percentages among the four verbal communication forms were compared, the results were as follows:

Type of verbal communication	Percentage
Listening	42%
Talking	32%
Reading	15%
Writing	11%

Thus, Rankin's study concluded that, among adults, listening is the form of verbal communication most frequently employed during an average waking day.

Several other investigations have been conducted more recently

---

* The phrase used throughout this text to refer to involved message receivers is *active listeners*. This phrase and its opposite, *passive listeners*, will be defined later in this chapter (see page 9).

which have confirmed Rankin's findings. Bird (1953) investigated verbal communication behavior of students in a women's college. The coeds indicated that listening consumed a significant portion of their verbal communication time—42 percent during an average day. Eighty-two percent of the coeds indicated that listening was equal to or more important than reading as a factor contributing to success in college. Bird (1954) also studied listening by dieticians. That group rated listening as the most important verbal communication skill in their job, followed in order by speaking, writing, and reading. The survey indicated that, during the course of their job, dieticians spent three times as much time listening as using any other form of verbal communication. An additional study by Breiter (1957) investigated the percentage of time housewives spend in the four types of verbal communication. They reported that they spent 48 percent of their verbal communication time listening, 35 percent speaking, 10 percent reading, and 7 percent writing. It can be seen that Bird's and Breiter's studies support the earlier findings of Rankin's investigation.

Turning to a related area of research, several studies have demonstrated that students spend more time listening in the classroom than teachers realize. In a study by Wilt (1949), elementary teachers were asked to estimate the time they thought pupils spent listening during an average school day. The results were then compared with the actual number of minutes students were involved in listening to these same teachers in the classroom. The findings indicated that the pupils listened about twice as much (158 minutes) as the teachers estimated they had been required to listen (77 minutes). It is interesting to note that the students spent 54 percent of their total classroom listening time listening to the teacher. A similar study by Markgraf (1957) found that high school students listened approximately 46 percent of the time during an average school day; 66 percent of this time was spent listening to the teacher. (In English classes, 97 percent of the time was spent listening to the teacher.)

What can we conclude from these studies? First, that listening is an important form, if not *the* most important form, of verbal communication in which we engage. Second, that students are required to listen a lot, in fact more than teachers think they require them to listen. Third, that considerable amounts of listening time in the classroom are spent listening to the teacher. In light of these conclusions, it should be evident that listening is an important skill in both the classroom and daily life, and that it is advantageous to possess effective listening skills in order to meet listening demands placed on us every day.

Why Learn to Listen?

This question may be best answered by examining some of the reasons given for teaching listening at primary, secondary, and college levels. Petrie (1961) suggests several reasons why listening is taught. (1) As we have seen, listening is used more frequently than any other form of verbal communication, particularly in the classroom. (2) Listening ability is important to the development of other language arts skills. As will be discussed later in this chapter, listening can help build vocabulary, develop language facility, and improve language usage. (3) Listening is not a very efficient means of learning; therefore, additional training is needed in order to help students learn more efficiently through listening. Again, since much learning in the classroom depends on listening to the teacher, it is critical that the skills for listening parallel those for reading (the form of verbal communication for which most training is provided at the elementary level).

However, aside from these very pragmatic reasons for teaching listening, there are other good reasons why you should be concerned with improving your listening ability. Many of these involve personal rewards for the listener; the rewards vary with the type of listening engaged in. In a later section of this chapter, various sub-types of listening will be discussed. For the present, the rewards for two general sub-types of listening will be delineated—serious listening and social listening. Serious listening involves listening with a specific purpose to comprehend, understand, remember, evaluate, or criticize. It is the type of listening most frequently engaged in in classroom and public speaking settings. Social listening involves listening for the purpose of entertainment. It is the type of listening in which you engage when listening to the radio, television, or a concert.

SERIOUS LISTENING

The rewards for serious listening fall into two basic categories —general and specific. There are three basic general rewards which may be realized through serious listening. (1) Listening helps you *expand your knowledge.* You learn as you listen and gain new information. (2) You can develop *language facility and vocabulary* by listening, as will be discussed later in the text. Listening is the primary process through which language is learned. Consequently, vocabulary development is probably more dependent upon listening than upon reading. In addition, pronunciation of words is learned almost exclusively through listening. (3) Listening can enable you to *evaluate strong and weak points in a message.* At this point a differentiation must be made between active and passive listening (see next section). An active (involved) listener is one who listens with all of his senses. He immerses himself in the act of listening and attempts to screen out distracting stimuli and interference (see Chapter 2). When you listen actively you are in an excellent position to critically evaluate the strong and weak points in the message. The passive listener does not attempt to become involved in comprehending, understanding, or evaluating a message. He lets the speaker assume the major responsibility for the success of the communication. Since he is not in a position to critically evaluate a message, he does not receive this potential reward for listening.

There are also some specific rewards for serious listening, several of which are especially important to students. (1) Listening helps you *pass exams based on lectures.* You will recall that students often are expected to listen over half of the time to a teacher or professor. In certain subject matter areas the amount of listening time nears 100 percent. Much of the information presented by the instructor often appears later in some form on a quiz or exam. Therefore, it stands to reason that better listeners get higher grades on exams—and probably better grades in the course. (2) Listening can help you *save time and gain financial benefits.* Time and financial benefits are grouped together here because, as the old adage goes, "time is money." Several examples can demonstrate these rewards for listening. Assume that you are in an economics class and the instructor casually discloses, via an example of an economic principle, some current information about the stock market. Let us further assume that you make an investment based upon this incidental "tip" you received in class and make considerable financial gains. Although financial gains may occasionally be related directly to classroom listening, they accrue more often through listening outside the classroom. You can learn efficient ways of doing things to save time and money; you can pick up tips on how to save money, where to buy, and how to "cut red tape." (3) A specific advantage of listening that is particularly important to college students is that it is a *"shortcut to knowledge."* Many instructors provide in their lectures a concise summary of the main points in the textbook. In such classes, listening to the professor may even replace having to read the text. Listening also can prove to be a shortcut to knowledge when you have access to an expert on a given subject and you can ask him questions and get immediate answers. This process can be considerably more efficient than going to the library and reading through several volumes to obtain the same information. Examine your daily communication with others. What additional examples can you discover in which listening provides a shortcut to knowledge?

SOCIAL LISTENING

Social listening or listening for entertainment purposes also provides several rewards for the average listener. (1) Perhaps the most obvious reward is the *increased enjoyment of aural stimuli.* Just as becoming more actively involved in sports increases your enjoyment of sports, becoming an active listener increases listening pleasure. An album of "hard rock" music played so loudly it shakes the pictures on the walls provides considerable pleasure for many listeners. The beat and the combinations of sounds often provide as much enjoyment as the lyrics. (2) Listening also helps to *enlarge your experience.* In other words, you can examine (perhaps even vicariously experience) through aural channels, ideas and events which have occurred to other people without actually experiencing these events personally. For example, listening to a Mexican-American talk about his experiences in the New York City ghetto can provide you with deep insights into human experience not available through personal experience or through reading or other secondary sources of information. (3) Listening helps to *expand your interests.* If you, as an active listener, listen to a wide variety of interesting lectures, plays, radio-TV programs, and musical selections, your interests are automatically broadened and deepened. (4 and 5) The next reward for social listening is actually twofold. First, some types of listening can help *decrease tension.* This point is reinforced by the old adage, "music can soothe the savage beast." A second, related reward is that listening has a *therapeutic value.* Much research in clinical psychiatry and psychology has suggested the value of music and other sound stimuli as relaxation "therapy" for normal healthy people, and particularly for mentally disturbed patients (for example, see Ruesch, 1948). It has been discovered time and time again that dramatic readings, music, and other related aural stimuli tend to reduce tension and produce positive therapeutic values for the majority of active listeners. (6) Listening helps to *expand your awareness of cultural and ethnic influences.* By listening to music, plays, and speeches and by talking informally with people of different races and cultures, you can identify important elements related to your culture and the culture of others. This can help you see in a clearer perspective those mores, habits, and values existing in your own ethnic group and culture that are unique, as well as those shared by others. (7) Listening can help you *mature socially.* The emphasis is now shifted from listening in the context of music, speeches, or entertainment to conversations in social settings. It is through listening and responding to others that you gain social skills necessary for survival. This reward is very closely related to the next point. (8) Listening can help you *improve your personality* or your "image" held by other people. A good listener is always in demand. A listener who is thoughtful, critical, and courteous frequently is sought for companionship as well as for advice and counsel. This sets the stage for the final point. (9) Listening can help you *improve your self-confidence.* Through active listening you can become knowledgeable about more matters. In addition, you become more skilled in the social graces. These, plus the other benefits discussed, can help build your self-confidence as a person—that is, build a "deeper," more interesting person with much to contribute to conversation.

It should be emphasized that the rewards related to social and serious listening assume that the listener, first, is actively involved in the listening process and, second, is engaging in *desirable* listening behaviors. Later on in the text, several techniques for building desirable listening qualities and skills will be examined and discussed, along with a variety of specific listening problems.

Types of Listening

Listening has been classified in a variety of ways by communication scholars. Classifications have differed because interests, perceptions, and philosophical backgrounds differ among authors. Several different classifications are included below in an attempt to provide an overview of several of the different ways in which listening has been viewed. Each classification (e.g., active-passive) represents a specific way in which listening theorists and authors have chosen to discuss the listening process. Note that some classifications are essentially bi-polar (they represent variables at opposite ends of the same continuum), while other classifications are "topical" in nature (they do not necessarily range along a single continuum).

ACTIVE-PASSIVE

Before the two major types of listening in which people engage are discussed, the difference between active and passive listening should be reviewed. Barbara (1957, p. 12) differentiates between active and passive listening in the following manner:

> In the former, the individual listens with more or less his total self—including his special senses, attitudes, beliefs, feelings and intuitions. In the latter, the listener becomes mainly an organ for the passive reception of sound, with little self-perception, personal involvement, gestalt discrimination, or alive curiosity.

Passive listening, for purposes of this text, refers to those forms of listening in which many people engage simply because they happen to be present when someone else is talking (or music is playing, etc.). In other words the potential receiver of the message is minimally, if at all, concerned about the listening process. This type of listening is barely more than hearing (see Appendix A)—it simply involves receiving the sound stimuli and letting them evoke conscious thoughts sporadically, but not consistently.

The type of listening upon which this text focuses is active listening—involved listening with a purpose (e.g., to comprehend, evaluate, enjoy, etc.). Active listening accompanies the implementation of desirable listening skills.

Active listening can occur in one of the two settings previously mentioned—social (usually informal) and serious (usually formal). An attempt will be made to distinguish between these two general types of listening behaviors.

SOCIAL-SERIOUS

Social listening is most frequently employed in an informal nonstructured communication setting. It often is associated with conversation or entertainment. The following sub-types of social listening may be engaged in:

Appreciative listening. Appreciative listening involves such activities as recognizing tone and mood, appreciating speaker's style, interpreting character from a dialogue, visualizing images from music or message, listening for rhythm in speech or music, understanding the effect of the rest of the audience on the listener's reactions, and understanding the effect of the speaker's vocal quality and gesture on the listening process (see Early, 1954). An example of appreciative listening is listening to a poem read aloud, a concert, a story, a play, a TV program, or similar type of aural message. In this type of listening the message receiver gleans some sort of satisfaction or gratification from involving himself actively in the listening process.

Conversational listening. This type of listening differs from most other forms in that it involves two-way communication (see Chapter 2). One must switch from the role of the listener to the role of speaker and back to listener again. Conversational listening may approximate serious listening in some settings. Generally, it is classified as social because of the informal settings in which it usually occurs. It is critical to remember that in order to become a good conversationalist, you also must be a good listener. Think about it!

Courteous listening. Courteous listening also involves conversation but is generally practiced in communication settings in which you are primarily serving as the listener. Being a courteous

listener is difficult, because in many settings you probably are as interested (or more interested) in talking as you are in listening. However, in courteous listening—such as trying to counsel a friend in trouble, or serving as a sounding board for a friend's ideas—you are expected to accept the responsibility of listening with an open mind and of giving positive feedback and reinforcement to the person who is talking.

Listening to indicate love or respect. This type of social listening is often neglected. It is the type of listening that takes place when a parent listens to a child say something which may not be important to the parent but is extremely important to the child. The mere showing of attention to the child is often a reward or reinforcement (in the context of learning theory), whereas the lack of listening, whether intended or not, may serve as punishment.* Another example of listening that represents respect is in the classroom. If teachers are too busy or have too tightly structured the class to listen to their students, a refusal or inability to listen may be perceived as "punishment." If a teacher is willing to listen to his students and let them express their ideas and points of view, students feel the teacher is interested in them as individuals. Listening by the teacher also can be used to reinforce communication behaviors of students such as waiting one's turn to speak, politeness, correct grammar, and so forth.

Serious listening may be either selective or concentrated.† *Selective listening* involves listening only to segments of a message—either at random or on some predetermined basis. In other words the listener alternates between active and passive listening. *Concentrated listening* involves listening to the entire message and attempting to comprehend all of its aspects and, in essence, everything that was said. In some settings (such as in class) it is desirable to be a concentrated rather than a selective listener. In other settings, selective listening not only may be appropriate but may save you

---

* "Punishment," in this context, is used as learning theorists employ it —a response which tends to *inhibit* behavior, rather than let the behavior occur or promote or encourage (reinforce) it.
† Of course, social listening also may be both selected and concentrated. However, this distinction is less important with regard to social listening behaviors.

from wasting your energy trying to assimilate "worthless" information. Unfortunately, some listeners do not realize they are being selective as they listen. Selective listening is often a conditioned process resulting from poor listening habits. If you discover you frequently tend to be a selective listener, examine the consequences of this behavior. Attempt to develop skills of concentrated listening so you can use them when appropriate. This will involve retraining and considerable practice. (See Chapters 4 and 5.)

Serious listening may be divided into two sub-categories—critical and discriminative listening.

Critical listening.   Basically, critical listening is listening in which the message receiver attempts to analyze the evidence or ideas presented by the speaker and makes critical judgments about the validity and quality of materials presented. Critical listening involves a variety of skills, such as distinguishing between fact and opinion, distinguishing between emotional and logical arguments, detecting bias and prejudice, evaluating the speaker's arguments, recognizing propaganda (see Chapter 6), drawing inferences and making judgments, and evaluating sales "gimmicks" (see Early, 1954). Most critical listening occurs in public speaking settings.

Discriminative listening.   Discriminative listening is listening for the purpose of understanding and remembering. This type of listening involves such skills as understanding meaning of words from context, understanding the relationship of details to main points, following steps when given directions, following the sequence of the message (e.g., plot development, character development, speaker's argument), listening for details, listening to a question with an intent to answer, recognizing the speaker's purpose, recognizing repetition of the same idea in different words, repeating what has been heard, and taking notes and outlining (see Early, 1954).

The most common example of discriminative listening is that which ideally should take place in the classroom. There are four levels of classroom listening in which students (or other listeners) may engage: (1) *Attentive listening.* The primary goal of attentive listening is to attend to the message, that is, pay attention. This is a rather superficial level of listening but is considerably better than not paying attention at all. (2) *Retentive listening.* The second level of listening involves a further commitment to the speaker than mere attention. It involves an attempt to comprehend and remember the message being presented. You may elect to employ various mnemonic (memory) devices to aid you in remembering what the speaker said. Among the more common are: associations of names with people's physical or personality attributes; grouping ideas into classes of three items each and imposing an organizational structure familiar to the speaker on a list of items to be learned or memorized (for example, let the rooms in your home mentally represent different points to be remembered). (3) *Reflective listening.* In reflective listening the listener not only attends and retains information but mentally evaluates the information in his mind and draws inferences and relationships about the material. Reflective listening involves the successful coupling of active listening skills with active mental processes related to information processing and evaluation. (4) *Reactive listening.* The final level of discriminative listening is reactive, in which the message receiver attends to the information, attains it, reflects upon it, and gives verbal or nonverbal feedback to the speaker indicating his evaluation of or response to the message that was presented. Note that reflective and reactive listening take place in critical as well as discriminative listening settings.

Although it is often useful to talk about listening in terms of some of the various classification schemes discussed above, it should be emphasized that a given listening event rarely can be characterized adequately by only one type of listening. For example, at a dinner party you may, as your interest level fluctuates, alternate between active and passive listening. In addition, you may switch from serious to social listening and back several times throughout the evening—for example, when you stop talking about golf with your roommate and begin talking with him about the exam scheduled for Tuesday. In other words, listening is a *process.* By its very nature it is constantly in a state of change. Keep in mind that in a "typical" listening setting listeners usually engage in a variety of listening types of levels at one time.

Summary

In this chapter the importance of the listener in the total communication process was illustrated. It was emphasized that the mere presence of a message receiver does not guarantee that communication will occur. The message receiver must be an active listener in order for communication to be successful.

People spend a large proportion of their waking day listening. Estimates run from about 50 percent to almost 100 percent in some classroom settings. Teachers often are not aware that students are required to listen to them as much as they do.

Several rewards may be received from active listening in both social and serious listening settings. Rewards for listening in serious settings include expansion of knowledge, vocabulary development and language improvement, ability to evaluate messages, passing examinations, saving time, accruing financial benefits, and short-cutting acquisition of knowledge. Listening in social settings may result in the following rewards: increased enjoyment of aural stimuli, enlargement of experiences, expansion of interests, decreasing of tension, relaxation, expansion of cultural awareness, social maturation, personality improvement, and increased self-confidence.

Listening may be classified in a variety of ways. Some different types of listening include: active, passive, social (including appreciative, conversational, courteous, and listening to indicate love and respect), and serious (including critical and discriminative listening). There are four different levels of listening in the classroom: attentive, retentive, reflective, and reactive listening. Classroom listening involves both critical and discriminative listening.

QUESTIONS FOR DISCUSSION

1. What factors in the communication environment contribute to making listeners more passive than active? How can listeners alter the environment for their benefit?

2. What process should a passive listener follow in order to become a more active listener?

3. What rewards, other than those mentioned in this chapter, can be gained from active listening?

4. What relationships exist between listening in social and serious settings? What are the primary differences?

5. What unique demands does the classroom environment place upon the listener?

6. What problems may result from failure to listen effectively?

Chapter 2

AN ANATOMY
OF THE
LISTENING PROCESS

Content Objectives for Chapter 2

Upon completion of this chapter, you should be able to:

(1) Define, orally or in writing, the term "listening," similar to the definition presented in the chapter.

(2) Draw a verbal-pictorial simplified model of the interpersonal communication process, identical to the one presented in the chapter.

(3) After drawing the model specified in Objective (2), define each term used to describe an element or process in the model.

(4) Draw a verbal-pictorial model of the listening process identical to the one presented in the chapter.

(5) After drawing the model specified in Objective (4), define each term used to describe an element or process in the model.

(6) Specify, in writing, at least two observations generated by the listening model, either similar to those presented in the chapter or original ones.

(7) Specify in writing at least three observations concerning the relationship between listening and learning, either similar to those presented in the chapter or original ones.

Before beginning this chapter, review some of the misconceptions about listening presented in the quiz at the beginning of the text, in order to recall what listening is *not*. The purpose of this chapter is to help clarify what listening *is*, but such a task is rather difficult. The examination of false assumptions regarding listening provides some help in understanding the workings of the listening process.

This chapter provides a description of communication and listening processes followed by a set of reasonable hypotheses concerning the nature of listening. The descriptions and hypotheses are reasonable assumptions—not "facts." Because of limited research and validated theory in the area of listening, the ideal of providing an organized set of "facts" about listening is not yet attainable.

In Chapter 1 some reasons for listening and some types of listening were discussed. At this point it is necessary to define the term "listening" more precisely. Most people use the term in a casual sense; in everyday conversation it is often used synonymously with the word "hearing." * But from reading the previous chapter you know that listening encompasses much more than hearing. It involves a combination of several processes including attention, hearing, understanding, and remembering.

It is not as easy as you might guess to find a definition for listening that most people will agree upon. There is considerable disagreement concerning which elements and processes are encompassed by the term. There is similar disagreement when attempting to isolate the factors involved in the listening process. A few of the definitions of listening which have been proposed to date are:

. . . an analysis of the impressions resulting from concentration where an effort of will is required (Tucker, 1925)

. . . the attachment of meaning to oral symbols (Nichols, 1948)

. . . the ability to understand and respond effectively to oral communication (Johnson, 1951)

. . . the process of relating the spoken language in terms of past experiences and future courses of study (Barbe and Meyers, 1954)

* Although providing a technical explanation of the hearing process is not one of the primary purposes of this text, a brief discussion of the workings of the human ear is presented in Appendix A.

. . . the capacity of an individual to understand spoken language in the presence of a speaker (Still, 1955)

. . . a selective process by which sounds communicated by some source are received, critically interpreted, and acted upon by a purposeful listener (Jones, 1956)

. . . a definite, usually voluntary, effort to apprehend accoustically (Barbara, 1957)

. . . the act of giving attention to the spoken word, not only in hearing symbols, but in the reacting with understanding (Hampleman, 1958)

. . . the complete process by which oral language communicated by some source is received, critically and purposefully attended to, recognized, and interpreted (or comprehended) in terms of past experiences and future expectancies (Petrie, 1961)

It is obvious that the authors of these definitions differ in several instances regarding the kinds of symbols attended to by the listener. Some authors suggest that the symbols must be verbal, whereas others include nonverbal symbols such as sirens, door squeaks, horns, etc. as suitable stimuli for listening. Some definitions specify that listening must be face to face or "live." The position taken in this text is that listening is primarily face to face but also may be implemented via mass media such as radio, TV, film, records, and tape recordings. For the purpose of this text, listening will be defined operationally as *the selective process of attending to, hearing, understanding, and remembering aural symbols*. Thus, listening involves four separate but interrelated processes: attention, hearing, understanding, and remembering. These four terms will be discussed in detail later in this chapter. However, for the present, the following brief definitions will suffice. *Attention* refers to focused perception of visual and/or verbal stimuli (such as the speaker's message); *hearing* refers to the physiological process of receiving aural stimuli (note that seeing also may be a critical element in the listening process—see the listening model presented later in this chapter); *understanding* refers to the assignment of meaning to the messages received (hopefully similar meaning to that intended by the initiator of the message); and *remembering* involves the storing of meaningful information in the mind for the purpose of recalling it at a later time.

Listening and Communication

You probably already have been exposed to one or more "models" of human communication in a speech class or a communication text. The purpose of this section is primarily to review some of the basic components that are included in most models of interpersonal communication in order to place the role of the listener in context. For a more detailed description of communication models than is appropriate for this text see: Ross (1965); Wiseman and Barker (1967); and Ronald L. Smith, "Theories and Models of Communication Processes," in Barker and Kibler (1971). The simplified communication model presented on page 19 will serve as the basis for discussion.

Study the model * carefully. Refer to it often as you read this section. You will note that it is composed of several elements and processes which *appear* to be linear and independent of each other. The word "linear" suggests that the variables in the model assume an ordered relationship, in which one process precedes another, then another, and so on. This concept of linearity in a communication model is generally valid. However, it should be obvious that in certain instances human interpersonal communication may not represent a linear process but rather a process involving multiple transmission and receptions which occur almost simultaneously.

The appearance of independence (no overlap existing) among variables and processes also may be misleading if you merely examine the model without attempting to relate it to real life communication settings. Although the variables appear discrete (inde-

---

* The term "model" used in this context refers to a verbal-pictorial representation of a process—in this case, communication. The general use of the term "model" in the behavioral sciences is considerably more precise than it is defined here. Models in the behavioral sciences generally are used to help build systematic theories. Verbal-pictorial models referred to in this chapter are primarily for the purpose of providing visual representations of very complex processes—they help serve as educational aids in explaining communication and listening processes. It should be emphasized that these models are not "laws." They are based on some empirical foundations, but are primarily derived from observations and inferences.

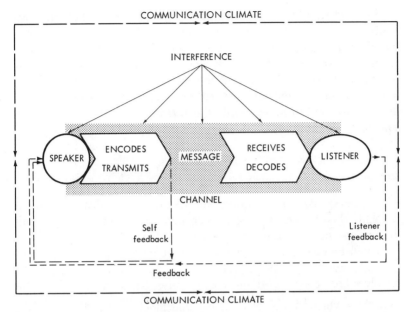

Figure 1. Simplified Communication Model

pendent) on the model, it should be understood that many of them in reality interact simultaneously. In order to separate or dichotomize many of them you would have to make arbitrary, and perhaps artificial, distinctions about where one process ends and another begins. Now, understanding that the communication process is not necessarily linear nor composed of independent processes, let us examine the variables included in the simplified Model of Communication.

(1) SPEAKER (TALKER, SOURCE, ORIGINATOR, ORIGINATING COMMUNICATOR, ETC.)

The speaker initiates the interpersonal communication process as a result of some perceived need to impart information or elicit a response. This need is often referred to as a *stimulus*. Stimuli may originate from within the speaker (internal stimuli) or from some outside source (external stimuli). Even though the term "speaker" is commonly used to describe the initiator of the message, it is understood that he may communicate through both verbal and non-verbal (such as visual) channels. The speaker may use gestures, facial expressions, and his physical appearance in addition to word symbols to communicate his message. As a student of listening, it is important to keep in mind that the primary reason a speaker transmits a message is to gain a specific response or a set of responses from a listener. In other words the *listener* holds the "key" to the speaker's success.

(2) Encoding

The speaker first encodes his thoughts and ideas into word symbols, bodily movements, and/or gestures which hopefully will be understood by a listener. The choice of symbols for communication will be determined to a great extent by the speaker's environmental, hereditary, and cultural influences. The encoding process involves both conditioned and cognitive responses on the part of the speaker. Successful communicators carefully encode their messages (that is, execute deliberate, cognitive decisions) when attempting to select symbols appropriate for the listener or audience.

(3) Transmission

Once the message symbols have been encoded, the speaker transmits them through a specific channel or channels to the listener. In human verbal communication, the transmitter uses a complex array of psycho-physiological bodily components (larnyx and pharnyx, lips, tongue, lungs, etc.) which lead to the production of speech sounds. In nonverbal (physical) communication the speaker transmits a message by means of an intricate system of muscles, nerves, and controlled bodily movements.

(4) Message

In most human communication, messages are, in essence, extensions of the speaker. In other words messages travel across time and space, imparting stimuli to the listener. In ideal communication, messages allow the speaker to gain a specific response from the listener with a minimum of mental and physical effort. Messages are often categorized according to their desired impact on the listener. (See Wiseman and Barker, 1967, for a complete description of message types.)

(5) CHANNELS

Channels are the pathways on which messages travel. In interpersonal communication the channels are usually light or sound waves. Visual and spoken messages are transmitted via these channels from the speaker to the listener and back. Channels are often referred to as media for communication.

(6) COMMUNICATION CLIMATE
(FIELD OF EXPERIENCE,
LIFE ORIENTATION)

The communication climate involves the sum total of hereditary and environmental influences for both the speaker and listener which have affected their individual personalities, language, and physical development. In addition, the communication climate includes the physical environment in which communication takes place. The climate is affected by long-range and immediate factors which may alter the probability that successful communication can occur.

Generally, it is necessary for some aspects of the speaker's communication climate to overlap similar aspects of the listener's communication climate with regard to the message being transmitted (e.g., both must have similar meanings for words used). Ideally, the communication climates for speaker and listener should be similar. This is rarely possible, so the speaker must make a concerted effort to adapt to the subjective communication of the listener, and the listener must do the same for the speaker. The speaker also must be aware that his own attitudes and behaviors may affect the listener's communication climate and, consequently, the listener's response. (For an additional discussion of this variable see Wiseman and Barker, 1967.)

(7) INTERFERENCE (NOISE)

In most communication settings some sort of noise (aural or visual) is present. The extent to which this "interference" is allowed to distort the message is somewhat a function of several factors, including the volume (loudness) of the message, the amount of light in the room, etc. But the most important fact to note at this point is that listeners may overcome the effects of message interference if they are aware of its potential distorting effects. In most settings interference can be controlled or compensated for by the speaker, by the listener, or by modification of the communication environment.

(8) Reception

At any given moment literally dozens of stimuli reach the listener from his immediate environment. Many of these stimuli are strong * (for example, a lecture by a teacher)—others are relatively weak (the noise of traffic outside the classroom). The process that involves receiving the stimuli through the senses is termed "reception." Bodily receptors include the ears, nose, eyes, tongue, and skin, as well as receptors beneath the skin which react to heat and pain. In most speech communication the primary receptors are the ears. It is important to note that of all stimuli received, only the strongest ones are transmitted to the brain and central nervous system for conscious thoughts and response. A process called discrimination (see the listening model later in this chapter) serves to screen out weak or irrelevant stimuli.

(9) Decoding

The decoding process is the reverse of the encoding processes previously discussed. It is the process in which the listener transforms the speaker's words and nonverbal symbols into meaningful thoughts and ideas. These thoughts and ideas take the form of electro-chemical impulses which are transmitted from the brain to the central nervous system (and, in some instances, the autonomic nervous system).

* "Strong" in this context refers primarily to the *relative importance* of the stimulus as perceived by the listener. Speakers may gain the listener's attention by such devices as talking louder or using startling language, but the strength of the stimulus is still defined in terms of the listener's perception.

(10) THE LISTENER

Since this entire text is about listening, there is little need to describe the listener in detail at this point. However, you should recall that the listener is more than just an absorber or receiver of a message. He has responsibility to respond to the speaker indicating the message has been understood (see Chapter 7). The terms "responder," "responding communicator," and "receiver" are often substituted for the term "listener." In a sense the first two terms may be more accurate in describing the role the receiver of a message should perform in the communication process.

(11) FEEDBACK

The response messages the listener transmits back to the speaker are often termed "feedback." * In a sense, at the feedback stage in the communication cycle the process is reversed and the listener becomes the message initiator. It is useful at this point to differentiate among some of the different types of feedback which indicate levels of comprehension on the part of the listener.

One type of feedback indicates that a message has been *understood* by the listener—it does not necessarily imply agreement. A second type of feedback suggests that the message, in whole or in part, was not received or understood. If a speaker asked you, "What is your name?" and you replied, "I'm taking Biology 304," this would be a clear example of this form of comprehension feedback. Your response indicated you did not understand the initial message. Remember that this type of feedback does not necessarily imply disagreement, it just indicates that the message was not correctly received, decoded, or interpreted. The third type of feedback is ambiguous in nature. It occurs when a listener transmits an unclear message back to the speaker; the listener may be interpreted as indi-

* This does not necessarily imply that the listener can make an immediate or direct response to the speaker. For example, when listening to radio or television, it is impossible to respond directly and immediately to the speaker. However, indirect or delayed responses may be made by buying products advertised, watching or listening to the program again, writing or calling the station, and so forth (see Chapter 7).

cating comprehension or noncomprehension. With ambiguous feedback it is the speaker's responsibility to determine whether or not the listener understood the message. A blank or noncommittal expression on the listener's face is the most obvious form of ambiguous feedback. This is especially prevalent in the classroom situation, when students sit and stare at the teacher who is trying to secure a response from the class. Listeners should try to avoid ambiguous feedback since it can lead to breakdowns in the communication process.

It is often confusing to classify feedback types, because the type of feedback you send may be perceived inaccurately by the speaker. It is difficult to know whether or not your intended feedback is being interpreted correctly. Chapter 7 provides several suggestions to help improve the effectiveness of your feedback.

It also should be noted that, in addition to the three types of interpersonal feedback the listener transmits to the speaker, the speaker also transmits some forms of feedback to himself. The speaker can hear his own words, and, in some instances, actually "feel" the words as they are forming in his oral cavity. This self-feedback, coupled with feedback from the listener, helps the speaker to correct his message and tends to make it more understandable for the listener.

To the student of listening, the model of communication should graphically illustrate the point that, in many instances, the speaker and listener change roles from moment to moment. This is especially true in informal conversations and small group discussions. It is not uncommon for a listener to respond to a speaker's message, then add some additional comments which begin a new "cycle" of communication. The speaker and listener must be willing to adapt and exchange roles when necessary, realizing the different responsibilities accompanying each role.

A Model of the Listening Process

Having examined the communication process in its entirety, let us now focus our attention specifically on listening. The diagrams on the following pages should help clarify the role of the listener in communication and provide a conceptual view of the listening

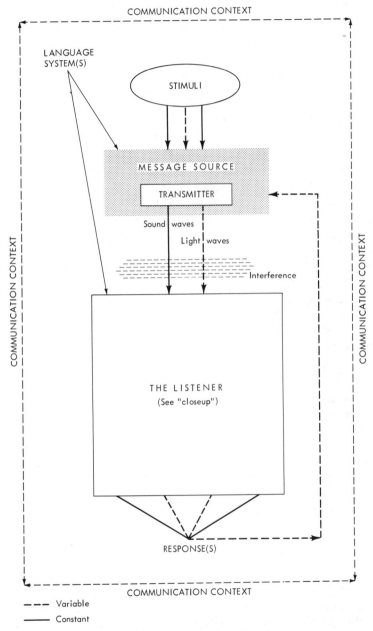

Figure 2. A Listening Model

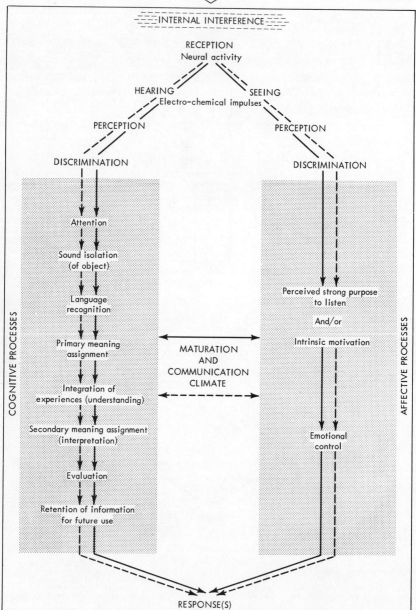

Figure 3. A "Closeup" View of the Listener

process. Begin by examining the model carefully, then refer back to it often!

First, note the conventions used in the model. A solid unbroken line represents elements or processes that are "constant" in the majority of listening situations. A broken or dotted line represents elements or processes that are "variables." In other words, the "constants" are present more often than not in the listening process, whereas "variables" may or may not be present, depending upon the specific nature of the listening setting.

It also is important to remember that, like the model of communication, this model appears to be linear, two dimensional, and composed of independent variables and processes. However, listening is rarely linear and is definitely not a two-dimensional process; it is a very complex multi-dimensional activity, as are most communication-related activities. Similarly, the actual time span between interrelated processes appears equal in the model, whereas in reality there may be a very long, or an infinitely short period of time between them. In some cases certain processes may occur simultaneously, even though in the model they appear to be in a definite sequence. (Note: The "closeup" view of the listener is an integral part of the Listening Model. The reason the closeup view appears on a separate page is for the sake of clarity and to avoid visual complexity in the model.)

Each process and variable will be discussed separately.

(1) COMMUNICATION CONTEXT

The large broken line which forms a square encompassing the entire model of listening represents the setting in which the listening behavior is executed. The inclusion of context as an important element in listening presupposes that words and actions are not constant or independent, but that their meaning is determined in part by prior understandings, events, and agreements. The context may be defined in terms of environment, listener attitudes, speaker attitudes, or similar variables. The listening process must be examined in the context in which it occurs because context determines, to a large extent, the meanings the listener will attach to the speaker's verbal or nonverbal symbols.

The variables that contribute to the communication context

are similar to those that comprise the communication climate in the total process of communication. These include hereditary, environmental, and cultural influences which converge to make the listener a "unique" individual. An example of environmental context might be the difference between classroom and dormitory rooms. We know, for example, that many teachers react differently to topics discussed in class than to the same topics discussed in an informal session with their students.

The listener's attitudes precede his listening in most instances. They help supply the listener with motives, intents, and points of view he may attribute to the speaker. These prior attitudes often determine the listening context entirely because the listener views the speaker's motives in his own subjective framework—regardless of the objective reality of the situation. Horowitz (1968, p. 9) suggests that "to the extent that attitude is cognitive it is also civilized, rational, deliberate, thoughtful, considerate, and aware, for it does include belief and knowledge. But, attitude is mostly irrational and frequently unconscious. Unfortunately, if you don't like someone you have made it almost impossible for him to say sensible things with good motives." What we listen to depends, to a considerable degree, on our perception and discrimination processes, discussed below, and both of these processes are affected to a considerable degree by attitudes.

(2) Language Systems

Before most types of listening can occur there must be an agreed upon language system as the basis for communication. In most cases the language system will be a verbal one which will be understood by both the speaker and the listener. However, the language system may be nonverbal (for example, the language of the deaf). It also may be a combination of verbal and nonverbal languages agreed upon by two or more human beings through convention or through constant interaction with each other. For example, couples who have been dating for a long period of time tend to know from looking at facial expressions and other gestures whether the other partner is happy, sad, wants something, and so forth. This language, even though informal, is considered sufficient as a basis for listening behavior.

The important thing to remember about the role of the lan-

guage system in the listening process is that the speaker must have sufficient commonality of language with the listener to be understood. If this condition is not met, listening breakdowns will inevitably occur.

(3) STIMULI, SOUND AND LIGHT WAVES, AND INTERFERENCE

In all communication settings there must be a stimulus, or stimuli, to initiate a message. These stimuli, when decoded, serve to stimulate the message source (speaker) to communicate with the listeners. The two major classes of stimuli for speaking and listening are sound and light. Sounds are generally transmitted from a human organism or through a recording. The sound waves are affected by interference, resulting in varying degrees of distortion in the message. An example of such interference would be the roar of automobiles outside the window when a speaker is talking. This interference or "noise," as it is often termed, alters the sound waves by the time they are received by the listener and distorts the way in which they affect the nervous system of the listener. (See the previous discussion of interference accompanying the model of communication.)

The same principle of interference holds true with light waves, although usually not to such a great extent. Theoretically, total interference with light waves would result in darkness. However, except for rarefractions of light which cause some natural distortion in vision, there is little cause for concern with light wave interference.

These types of interference refer to sights or sounds that tend to *alter* messages. However, there is another type of interference, either visual or aural, which tends to distract attention from other primary messages in the communication setting. (See Wiseman and Barker, 1967, pp. 33-34.) For example, a very beautiful painting in a room may create visual interference among an audience. Similarly, in some communication settings the color of one's skin might create some visual interference and distract from the content of a message (for example, a white speaker talking to an all black audience). Regardless of whether interference alters a message or provides distractions from a primary message, it is important to be aware of its presence and to attempt "control" for it when possible.

Sound and light, then, provide primary "raw" stimuli for the listening process to occur. The "true" stimuli which prompt the speaker to want to communicate with the listener often reflect personal or social needs of the speaker. In the framework of learning theory, a stimulus tends to elicit a given response. This is diagramed S → R (Stimulus → Response). Recent learning theorists discuss what is termed "mediation" in learning. In mediated learning, instead of assuming a stimulus elicits an "automatic" response in an individual, it is suggested that organisms react to the stimulus according to their genetic and psychological compositions, and these variables affect or mediate the response which is given. This is diagramed S → O → R (Stimulus → Organism → Response). The stimulus to communicate is mediated by the speaker before he responds by composing and transmitting a message to the listener. The stimuli provided by the speaker's message to the listeners (in the form of words or nonverbal symbols) are, in turn, mediated by the listener before he responds (gives feedback) to the speaker.

(4) Transmitter(s)

The process of transmission was described briefly in the discussion of the communication model. Transmission, in human communication, generally stems from vibrations of the vocal folds in combination with vocal resonators and respiration activities. Nonverbal visual symbols are transmitted through movements and facial expressions, via muscles and nerves.

(5) Reception, Neural Activity, Hearing, and Seeing

From one point of view these are the first real components of the listening process. However, it is obvious that a message must first be transmitted before listening can occur. The process of reception in listening *primarily* involves hearing. It assumes the presence of a hearing organism which is adequately developed and in sufficient repair to assimilate stimuli transmitted through sound waves. (For a more detailed examination of the hearing process, see Appendix A.) When listening involves the variable of visual communication, the eyes also are message receptors. Seeing is thought by some to be a critical variable in listening, but the view in this text, stated earlier, is that listening may occur without seeing the message originator. Generally, a combination of hearing and seeing will cause the listener to add additional meanings to verbal messages but, by definition, the eyes are secondary receptors in the listening process. Remember, at this point in the listening process only message reception takes place. Listening does not occur until the received messages have been internalized, analyzed, and interpreted.

Once messages have been received, in the form of visual or aural stimuli, the stimuli initiate the flow of electro-chemical neural impulses to the brain and central nervous system which, when decoded (see the model of communication), cause the listener to begin thinking about or responding to the new stimuli.

(6) PERCEPTION
AND DISCRIMINATION

Perception is related to, but different from reception. Reception (hearing and seeing) is primarily a biological or physiological process. Perception is a combination of physiological (primarily neural) and mental processes (both cognitive and attitudinal). Perception involves screening of raw stimuli in order to select those which are of sufficient strength or importance to stimulate thought.* It is, in essence, a filtering process and has been described figuratively as a screen. The perception process filters out irrelevant stimuli and retains only the most important ones. Using the analogy of sifting sand through a screen, the smallest particles are allowed to slip through but the biggest (most important) particles remain for examination. Several studies in the area of perception have concluded that the louder, the more relevant, and more novel the stimuli, the more likely they are to be perceived by the listener. Consequently, these stimuli which are perceived are subjected to preconscious or conscious cognitive and attitudinal processing by the listener.

---

* This process is often termed "selective perception." Brunner (1957) refers to perception as the "Gating Process," which implies a filtering of stimuli before they reach the brain. This is analogous to "gatekeeper" in small groups and organizations, who serve as "screeners" of information coming into the group and leaving the group.

The learned or conditioned process of discrimination interacts with the process of perception. Some theorists (e.g., Horowitz, 1968) refer to the discrimination process as "channeling." Perceptual discrimination is primarily a learned behavior which makes us attend to certain types of stimuli more readily and completely than to others. For example, if you hear your name in a given message you are conditioned to attend to this message more readily than if the message contained the name of a stranger. Similarly, symbols which have little or no meaning to us, as a result of our past experiences, education, etc., often do not receive our attention and therefore have little or no effect on us as listeners. Perceptual discrimination takes place at both cognitive and affective (emotional or attitudinal) levels of listening. (Listening usually involves a combination of cognitive and emotional elements.) Now let us examine some of the sub-processes involved in the cognitive aspect of listening.

(7) COGNITIVE PROCESSES

(a) **Attention.**   Attention is a necessary condition for listening once a message has been perceptually discriminated. The message must be given conscious attention, that is, it must be allowed to supersede all other competing sounds and visual stimuli, in order to be comprehended. Attention is a factor of prime concern for speakers because research has indicated that adults attend to specific stimuli for very short periods of time (normally from about 5 to 25 seconds). Listeners who are aware of natural tendencies to shift attention from one stimulus to another can increase the length of their attention span through concentration, practice, and self-discipline. Once a stimulus gains cognitive attention, a succession of mental processes operate in such "rapid fire" order that it is somewhat misleading to talk about them as discrete processes. However, as was noted previously, this is a limitation which is inherent in verbal-pictorial models.

(b) **Sound Isolation.**   Before cognitive information processing occurs, human beings first perceive isolated sounds or groups of sounds which must be placed in some order and context before they are recognized as meaningful word symbols.

(c) **Language Recognition.** After the isolated sounds are perceived, the patterns of sounds may then be cognitively assimilated. When the assimilated isolated sounds are recognized in a specific context, a meaningful set of symbols (i.e., language) becomes discernible.

(d) **Primary Meaning Assignment.** At this point, the recognized word symbols are assigned what might be termed the first level of meaning. This is a level of meaning which primarily is a result of conditioned responses to sets of word symbols. Little deliberation or conscious attempt on the part of the listener to critically examine the meaning of the word symbols is present at this stage.

(e) **Integration of Experiences.** After the listener assigns primary meanings to the word symbols, he then begins to integrate past experiences which bear on the symbols for which he has previously attached meaning. The integration of experiences may occur over a long period of time or it may take place in a split second.

(f) **Secondary Meaning Assignment (or Interpretation).** After experiences are allowed to alter the primary meanings, the listener may still attach deeper or secondary levels of meaning to the symbols. At this stage the message may or may not be understood correctly by the listener; but he subjectively believes he has attached the "correct" meaning (the meaning intended by the speaker) to the message being transmitted.

(g) **Evaluation.** After the listener feels he understands what the message means, he usually attempts to evaluate it, consciously or subconsciously, in light of his value structure, attitudes, and beliefs. His evaluation may or may not be expressed in the form of a response to the originator of the message; but it is, nevertheless, useful in helping shape his reaction toward future messages related to the recently received message. Evaluation poses a special problem in the context of effective listening behavior. In Chapter 4 it is emphasized that it is undesirable to *prematurely* evaluate the worth of a message. It is more desirable to wait until you have all the information available and then make a careful and critical evaluation. In addition, it is unwise to evaluate the personality of the speaker instead of his message. This leads to invalid evaluations in many instances. The inclusion of evaluation as an element in the listening process indicates the necessity for critical assessment of the content of a message.

(h) **Retaining Information for Future Use.** If the purpose of the speaker in transmitting the message is to inform or teach, then listeners should make an effort to retain the information for future reference. This internalization of information is generally a cognitive process and demands considerable conscious effort on the part of the listener. Communication breakdowns commonly occur because listeners do not succeed in remembering a sufficient proportion of information to execute necessary tasks. Listeners often think that they will retain information for a long period of time after hearing a message once. We know from examining the learning-forgetting curve that about 90 percent of the information that we gain through hearing will not be remembered unless something "cues" the information up at a later date. We also must keep in mind that what information we do retain may become distorted, changed, or reordered over time. Consequently, the information you remember may not represent the same message you heard initially. In order to increase the percentage you can remember accurately, you must make a deliberate *conscious* attempt to retain information for future use. This involves *active* listening. Let us now examine several variables which relate to the affective (attitudinal or emotional) state of the listener.

(8) Affective Processes

(a) **Perceived Purpose to Listen.** After perceptual discrimination has taken place in the emotional aspect of listening, the listener ideally should perceive a *strong purpose for listening.* What constitutes a strong purpose for one listener may not constitute a purpose for another. It is partially the responsibility of the speaker to make the message appear vital or purposeful so the listener will want to continue listening. An *active* listener will examine his previous experiences with the speaker's topic and attempt to generate internally a strong purpose for a message. Research has indicated that motivation is a vital component in the listening process, and that a genuine interest in what the speaker says adds considerably to the understanding and retention of information (see Mullin, 1957).

(b) **Intrinsic Motivation.** A major variable contributing to the presence of a perceived strong purpose for listening is *intrinsic motivation.* If the speaker does not have a stimulating style of delivery or a particularly interesting topic, an active listener can still try to generate reasons why it might be important, profitable, or appropriate to listen. Some such reasons have been discussed previously in Chapter 1 in the section on Rewards of the Listening Process.

(c) **Emotional Control.** Emotional control in listening is often important because heightened emotions, both positive and negative, can inhibit listening effectiveness. Where such emotions as fear, anger, hostility, anxiety, or jealousy are present, message perception is often affected. Intended meanings are inaccurately interpreted and information distortion becomes even more of a problem than occurs in "normal" communication settings. The presence of negative emotions primarily tends to: (1) reduce comprehension (because the mind is "racing" with other thoughts); (2) divide perception time between the speaker's message and the listener's thoughts (causing listening effectiveness to decrease); and (3) cause the listener's motivation to continue listening to decrease (because it is painful to listen). Effective speakers attempt to control the negative emotions they impart to listeners. If listeners are aware of the potential impact of negative emotions on their own listening behavior, they may be able to compensate for (control) the effect, though not completely eliminate it

Positive emotions (joy, anticipation, etc.) also may inhibit listening effectiveness. The presence of these emotions in great degrees tends to create mental distractions for listeners and makes it difficult for them to concentrate.

(9) MATURATION AND COMMUNICATION CLIMATE

A variable which interacts with both cognitive and emotional processes in listening is maturation. Maturation is the most important variable in the listener's communication climate (see the model of communication). At a given point in time, children become capable of attending to verbal messages and understanding them—often as early as 10-12 months of age. At another point in time—probably earlier than one year of age—children begin to understand visual nonverbal messages. Listening demands, at the very least, these basic levels of maturation. However, listening skills may be refined with appropriate practice, and the level of maturation of the listener will, in part, determine how effectively he can integrate all of the cognitive and emotional skills demanded of an active listener. In addition to maturation, all other variables which serve to shape the listener's communication climate also interact with the cognitive and affective processes.

(10) RESPONSE(S)

In most communication settings a response from the listener back to the speaker is not only desirable but necessary. As was noted previously, a direct response may not be necessary or possible when one is listening to certain types of stimuli such as music, radio-TV broadcasts, and so forth. However, it is important for the listener to take advantage of an opportunity to provide feedback, especially if he is not sure he has correctly interpreted the whole of the message. Feedback in interpersonal communication is vital because it allows the speaker immediately to correct or explain his message more fully.

Keep in mind that all of the elements involved in the listening process interact. Most, but not all of them, occur in the majority of "normal" listening situations. Remember that the major elements of the listening process are receiving the message, attending to, perceiving, processing, and understanding the message, and retaining elements of the message for future use. Response (feedback) to the speaker is not only desirable but extremely important for both speaker and listeners.

In trying to apply the listening model to your own listening behavior do not attempt to "pigeonhole" the variables (i.e., force variables into classes where they do not logically fit). Use the elements and variables delineated in the model to help you better understand the complex dynamic nature of the listening process.

Some Observations about Listening
Generated by the Listening Model

Having examined the entire listening model, you now should be able to describe the listening process and label elements and variables within the process as you begin to analyze listening behavior.

In addition, by viewing the model of listening at this rather abstract level, you can begin to postulate some hypotheses about listening and predict factors that contribute to listening success. Since there is no established listening "theory" at present (just a series of principles based primarily on observation and, to some extent, on research), you should feel free to speculate and experiment with the manipulation of variables in an attempt, first, to understand more completely the listening process, and second, to improve your own listening behavior.

Below are several observations about the listening process which appear reasonable. The list is by no means exhaustive, but it does reflect the type of speculations that may be made by engaging in some serious thinking, analysis, observation, and research about the listening process.

(1) *Meaning is not transmitted in oral communication—just aural and visual stimuli. Thus, meanings listeners attach to messages are based on inferences—not facts.* This hypothesis is almost a self-truth. We know that, though speakers process specific meanings for word symbols they transmit, the words themselves may not hold the same meanings for listeners. The degree to which the listener's meaning is accurate depends on a variety of factors including: listener's acquaintance with the speaker (knowledge of a speaker's past experiences bearing on the message, knowledge of his vocabulary, motivations, drives, etc.); speaker's ability to project what symbols will be meaningful to the listener; and motivation to listen carefully (i.e., perceived purpose plus generated intrinsic motivation). Unless both speaker and listener are actively concerned about the problem of reaching common agreement on the meanings for word symbols, there is a high probability that communication breakdowns will occur.

(2) *Listening is a form of intrapersonal communication.* In

other words, the process of listening is a process of communicating within one's self in response to an external stimulus. (See Barker and Wiseman, 1966a.) Intrapersonal communication is an active, ongoing process—not a passive static process. In the context of intrapersonal communication, listening involves perception, storing, processing, analyzing, and evaluation, which lead to a response through interpersonal communication (feedback). Viewing listening as a form of intrapersonal communication emphasizes the active nature of the process and exemplifies the close relationship between listening and the entire communication cycle.

(3) *Expectations of the listener contribute significantly to what he hears, comprehends, and interprets.* The listening model discussed the role of maturation on listening, as well as the assignment of meaning on the basis of past experiences. The listener's past communication climate has helped condition his perception of the immediate listening setting, the speaker, and the message being transmitted. If he is not careful to compensate for these perceptions, he may hear what he *thought* the speaker was going to say, rather than what he *actually did say.* By maintaining continued awareness that expectation can cause potential problems in communication, you should be better able to hear the message the speaker really is sending, rather than the message you think he is going to send.

Some Observations about Listening and Learning

Most listening scholars recognize early a direct relationship between the reception of aural stimuli and learning. In fact, learning and listening are so closely interrelated that the two processes frequently are confused.

Perhaps the relationship between listening and learning is most evident in the classroom setting. Not only do students receive over half of the information they are to learn through listening, but teachers also use listening as reward or punishment * in the class-

---

* The terms "reward" and "punishment" are used in a more general sense here than some learning theorists might prefer. However, this generalized conception of the terms appears to be more appropriate in light of the purposes of this section.

room. When the teacher attends to a student's verbal communication it can serve as a reward, or reinforcer, if it has been previously established that the teacher will listen only under specified favorable conditions (for example, she must be addressed in the proper manner, at the proper time, and so forth). Similarly, selective listening by the teacher can successfully modify classroom verbal and nonverbal behaviors. Some teachers, either consciously or inadvertently, use failure to listen as punishment by ignoring certain pupils who attempt to communicate to them.

There are other relationships which can be hypothesized about the effects of listening on learning and vice versa. The following observations appear tenable but still need to be supported or refuted by empirical research.

(1) *Listening is a conditioned (learned) behavior.* If this observation (hypothesis) is true, there are several implications for instruction. First, if listening is a conditioned behavior, it can be taught as well as learned. It would follow also that if listening is a conditioned response then adult listening patterns approach habits because they have been reinforced or punished over a relatively long period of time.

Secondly, some listening skills acquired early in life are affected significantly by cultural and environmental influences, especially in the home. Since few parents systematically attempt to teach their children to listen, the listening skills developed are primarily a result of imitative learning, and, unfortunately, parents often do not provide good models as listeners. The alternative to this hypothesis—that is, that listening is primarily a function of hereditary influences—appears very unlikely in light of present research and observation.

(2) *Listening habits (if they are conditioned or learned behavior) may be modified by instruction through reward or punishment.* Learning theory indicates that any learned behavior may be extinguished * through reward or punishment. Consequently, if observations (1) and (2) are sound, bad listening habits (see Chapter 4) may be extinguished and replaced by good habits (see Chapter 5). This hypothesis appears reasonable. Thus, it would appear that a systematic program of listening instruction should be developed to modify inappropriate listening behaviors.

---

* "Extinguishing" is defined by learning theorists as the systematic removal of the reinforcing conditions for specific learned behaviors.

(3) *Attention-motivation provides the initial stimulus for listening.* Viewing listening as a stimulus-response (S-R) or stimulus-organism-response (S-O-R) cycle, the stimulus must be strong enough to initiate listening on the part of the message receiver. The stronger the stimulus the more clearly will rewards or punishments be perceived for listening. In order for active listening to occur, it is desirable and necessary for the listener to maintain sufficient motivation to: (a) attend to the message; (b) want to understand the message; (c) internalize significant portions of the message; and (d) evaluate certain aspects of the message.

(4) *If punishment (perceived or real) for not listening is present, cognitive interference may be created which will, in reality, inhibit listening.* This observation, if substantiated, presents a real dilemma for those concerned with listening improvements. It suggests that when people are made to worry about their bad listening habits they may become even worse listeners. This problem could be critical for elementary teachers who continually stress listening by chiding, scolding, and making "examples" of children who do not listen. If this hypothesis is true, the solution is obvious, in light of learning theory. A program based on reinforcement of good listening skills by peers or other influential people, such as teachers, should be implemented in order to reinforce good listening habits. Through reinforcement of desirable listening habits, motivation to listen should be increased. (This is plausible, theoretically, because listening should become a more reinforcing experience!)

(5) *People tend to generalize across types of listening situations: they often do not discriminate differences among behaviors necessary for different types of listening under different conditions.* The implication in this observation is that different types of listening skills are needed in different listening settings. A close examination of the model of listening suggests that this is highly probable. For example, when both verbal and nonverbal cues are present, perceptual demands on and attention by the listener are considerably different than they are when only verbal cues are present. Similarly, when you listen to a set of directions that may save your life, the listening demands are substantially different from when you are listening to a message as a "captive audience." Perceived purpose for listening (coupled with intrinsic motivation) would alter the listening "style" in this instance. This hypothesis suggests that by analyzing each listening setting independently, listening skills may

be adopted accordingly. Consequently, listening should be enhanced and increased understanding should result.

Summary

Specification of a unified acceptable definition of the listening process is difficult. A variety of definitions of listening have been proposed, all with slightly different emphases. The definition presented in this chapter is "the selective process of attending to, hearing, understanding, and remembering aural symbols."

Listening must be analyzed in light of the entire communication cycle. The basic components in the process of interpersonal communication are: speaker, encoding process, transmission process, the message, channels, communication climate, interference, reception process, decoding process, listener, and feedback. Feedback from listener to speaker is a critical element in the communication process, for without feedback the cycle is not complete.

A model of the listening process enables us to examine the interrelationships among the various elements and processes. It also provides a framework for analysis and discussion of the process. The components of the listening process (as reflected in the model of listening presented in this chapter) include: communication context, language systems, stimuli to message source, sound and light waves, interference, transmission by message source, reception processes (hearing and seeing), neural activity, perception and discrimination, cognitive processes, emotional processes, maturation, and responses.

The model of listening allows us to make some tentative observations about the nature of the listening process. Three such hypotheses are: (1) Meaning is not transmitted in oral communication—just aural and visual stimuli; thus, the meanings listeners attach to messages are based on inferences—not facts. (2) Listening is a form of intrapersonal communication. (3) Expectations by the listener contribute significantly to what he hears, comprehends, and interprets.

Several additional observations may be made concerning the relationship between learning and listening. These include: (1) Listening is a conditioned (learned) behavior. (2) Listening habits (if they are conditioned or learned behaviors) may be modified by instruction through reward or punishment. (3) Attention-motivation provides the initial stimulus for listening. (4) If punishment (perceived or real) for not listening is present, cognitive interference may be created which will, in reality, inhibit listening. (5) People tend to generalize across types of listening situations; they do not discriminate differences among behaviors necessary for different types of listening under different conditions.

QUESTIONS FOR DISCUSSION

1. *In light of the models presented in this chapter, how much responsibility lies with the speaker to ensure that effective communication will take place? How much responsibility rests with the listener?*

2. *The model of communication presented in this chapter is a "simplified" description of the communication process. What factors or variables were omitted which would be found on a more complete communication model?*

3. *What additional variables, other than those specified in the listening model in this chapter, are involved in the listening process?*

4. *What is the nature of the relationship between learning theory and listening behavior?*

5. *What can be done to control the effect of negative emotions on listening?*

VARIABLES
WHICH MAY INFLUENCE
LISTENING BEHAVIOR

Content Objectives for Chapter 3

After completing this chapter, you should be able to:

(1) Specify, orally or in writing, at least four reasons why conflicting findings may occur among similar investigations concerning listening.

(2) Specify, in writing, at least ten listener characteristics, experiences, or abilities which relate (to a moderate or high degree) to listening effectiveness.

(3) Specify, in writing, at least three listener characteristics, experiences, or abilities which relate to a lesser degree to listening effectiveness.

(4) Specify, in writing, five or more speaker qualities which relate, at least moderately, to listening effectiveness.

(5) Specify, in writing, two or more message variables which relate, at least moderately, to listening effectiveness.

(6) Specify, in writing, three or more environmental variables which relate, at least moderately, to listening effectiveness.

(7) Specify, in writing, seven or more variables which have been found not to relate to listening effectiveness.

Listening researchers and social scientists have been concerned for some time with differentiating between good and poor listeners. Experimental and descriptive research projects have been executed in an attempt to isolate variables in listeners, speakers, messages, and environments which tend to affect listening comprehension and ability. Consequently, there is a considerable body of research data suggesting variables which tend to influence (or not influence) listening behavior.

Several summaries of listening research already exist. Some of the articles and monographs which synthesize research on listening include Petrie (1961); Keller (1960); Toussaint (1960); Duker and Petrie (1964); Thompson (1967); and Devine (1967). More complete summaries (in bibliographic—not synthesis form) may be found in Duker (1966) and Duker (1968). Because several "scholarly" summaries and synthesizing articles already exist, this chapter will present generalized findings in nontechnical language. References at the end of the chapter refer to selected research articles, monographs, and books related to the variable discussed in the section. The references cited at the end of the chapter are only examples of relevant research. They are not purported to be exhaustive lists of all of the articles available related to a given variable. When research was limited in a given area, attempts were made to fill in the gaps on the basis of observation and inferences.

Emphasis in this chapter is on interpretation as well as synthesis. However, you should keep in mind that interpretations of research data are subjective, i.e., they are subject to human inadequacies and biases. In addition, when conflicting findings are noted in the research literature—which often is the case—it is difficult to determine reasons for the differences reported and to infer which studies are more reliable, valid, and methodologically sound. Thus, the interpretations of research data which follow are clearly subjective and may conflict with interpretations of other scholars in some instances.

Four different categories of variables related to listening will be discussed in this chapter: (1) listener characteristics, experiences, and abilities, (2) speaker qualities, (3) message, and (4) environment. In each of the four sections research will be synthesized which suggests the relationship between the variable under consideration and listening. Differentiations are made in some sections between variables thought to be definitely related to listening and those thought to be slightly related.

The final section of the chapter discusses variables thought *not* to be related to listening ability. Many of these variables are often assumed to be related to listening ability but some research suggests little or no relationship.

I.* Listener Characteristics, Experiences, and Abilities

The variables discussed in this section relate to both physical and demographic characteristics of the listener as well as listener experience and mental abilities.

I.1. VARIABLES FOUND TO RELATE TO LISTENING SKILLS TO A MODERATE OR HIGH DEGREE

I.1.1 Sex. Results of several investigations comparing male and female listeners have indicated that males often are better listeners than females. Methodological considerations in investigations concerning this variable have been pointed out by some critics. The critics have raised questions as to whether differences noted were a function of true listening differences between males and females, or of uncontrolled testing situations, confounding variables, and so forth.

I.1.2 Age. Research dealing with the relationship between age and listening has indicated that, if a person has normal hearing, there is little relationship between age and ability to listen. However, there are some *age-related* variables which may influence listening. The primary one is attention span. Younger children have considerably shorter attention spans than young adults. (However, even adults have relatively short attention spans.) Similarly, when a person reaches old age and senility begins to occur, listening ability also may be affected negatively. (See Brown, 1959.)

Another area of research related to age and listening focuses on preference for listening over reading. In general, when a child

---

* References for each section and sub-section of this chapter are provided at the end of the chapter.

is about 12 or 13 he will begin to prefer reading over listening because he can read at his own speed, usually much faster than a speaker will talk. Younger children usually can listen more rapidly than they can read—thus they tend to prefer listening. Additional research on reading is presented later in this chapter.

I.1.3 Personality Characteristics. Considerable research investigating potential relationships between listening ability and personality has been conducted. Perhaps the most important finding in this area has been that ego involvement tends to reduce listening comprehension, whereas objectivity (i.e., reduced ego involvement) tends to increase listening ability. In addition, listeners who have personal worries or feelings of insecurity, or feel they are "doomed for failure," also tend to be poorer listeners than those who are optimistic and free from momentary worries. With regard to other personality characteristics, most investigations have concluded that there is less of a relationship between listening ability and personality than might be assumed intuitively.

I.1.4 Motivation and Curiosity. There has been considerable empirical research conducted to establish the relationship between motivation and listening ability. However, even on an intuitive basis it is rather obvious that motivation may affect listening ability. Listening is related to the learning process and research in learning clearly has established the relationship between motivation and the learning process. Therefore, it appears reasonable that motivation should affect one's ability to listen.

Two of the problems plaguing empirical research in the area of motivation and listening are: (1) motivation is an elusive construct to measure and (2) definitions of motivation often differ among researchers, making comparisons of results difficult.

I.1.5 Interest and Attitudes. Interest and attitudes are related closely to motivation and, therefore, generally may be assumed to relate to listening ability. However, research findings with regard to human interest and attitudes have been conflicting concerning their relationships to listening ability. Other factors which correlate with interest and attitudes (e.g., fear, love) may significantly increase or decrease one's ability to listen. For example, if you know you are to be tested on a certain section of a lecture, your ability to comprehend may increase slightly because of additional attempts on your part to gain the material. Whether or not this increased comprehension is a function of increased interest remains questionable. However, in general, we may assume that the more interesting you find orally presented material, the more likely you will be to listen to it.

I.1.6 Binaural Hearing.   Binaural hearing is similar to depth perception in seeing. It is the ability to discriminate the direction of the source of sound. Binaural hearing assumes that the ears are both operating properly and in "balance." There has been little research reported regarding the effects of binaural hearing on the ability to listen. However, it is reasonable to assume that in a situation in which only one sound source is present, listening would be unaffected whether or not one had good binaural hearing, but where two or more sound sources are present, the ability to hear binaurally would contribute significantly to the ability to discriminate among sound sources and concentrate on one more fully than the other. In addition, in situations where only one (primary) sound source is present, but where there are also other noises (such as air conditioner, external conversation, or a radio playing), it would appear that the ability to hear binaurally would enable the listener to suppress extraneous noises and listen more carefully to the major sound source.

I.1.7 Listener Fatigue.   When a listener is mentally or physically tired, his reduced attention span decreases his ability to listen proportionately. Listening fatigue can create a temporary hearing loss in which there is insufficient motivation to attend to and decode the stimuli transmitted by the speaker. Consequently, there is a strong relationship between listener fatigue and listening ability. The relationship is an inverse one; that is, the more fatigue a listener experiences, the less will be his ability to listen effectively.

I.1.8 Intelligence.   It is obvious that any mental activity—including listening—depends to a certain extent on intelligence. Research comparing listening tests (see Appendix C) with intelligence tests indicates there is a positive, but not high relationship between the scores. One explanation for the absence of a high correlation may be found in differences among the measuring instruments themselves (i.e., the tests). However, on the other hand it may be inferred logically that given a minimal level of intelligence, other components of the listening process are less directly related to intelligence than might be assumed. Some research does indicate that more intelligent people tend to comprehend more information from reading than from listening. Thus, listening and intelligence are related, but not to as high a degree as might be inferred intuitively.

I.1.9 Scholastic Aptitude and Achievement in High School. A considerable body of research has focused on the relationship between listening test scores and such indices of scholastic aptitude and achievement as aptitude tests, cumulative grade point averages (GPA), high school rank, and high school reading scores. The results have indicated that a moderate to high relationship usually exists between listening and grade point average as well as rank in high school class. Even higher relationships have been discovered between scholastic aptitude and listening. Relationships between listening, and reading ability and other indices are not consistent. This suggests that both listening and reading are probably related to intelligence which, in turn, is related to other indices of scholastic achievement, i.e., cumulative grade point average and rank in high school class. In summary, as might be expected, listening does relate moderately to scholastic achievement in high school and somewhat more to scholastic aptitude, but the relationships may be interpreted primarily as a function of intelligence rather than of "pure" listening skills.

I.1.10 Verbal Ability. The relationship between verbal ability and listening is similar in magnitude to the relationship between listening and intelligence. The relationship is a moderate but definite one. Research indicates that students who score higher on reading tests than listening tests also tend to score higher on language sections of IQ tests than on the sections involving listening skills. Thus, verbal ability and listening are related, but not to a high degree.

I.1.11 Vocabulary Size. Results of research concerning relationships between vocabulary size and listening are conflicting. However, the preponderance of evidence suggests the presence of a relationship between vocabulary size and listening comprehension skills. It is known from research and observation that effective listening skills help strengthen a listener's vocabulary.

I.1.12 Experience in Listening. This variable relates somewhat to the factor of age discussed previously, because listening experience increases with age. You will recall that the relationship between age and listening was not as high as might be predicted and, given a minimum age level at which one's vocabulary is developed sufficiently for listening, age has little effect on listening improvement.

Two investigations reported that listeners who score well on listening tests tend to engage more frequently in more difficult listening exercises (Nichols, 1943, and Tyler, 1946). This might indicate that it is not the *amount* of listening experiences that affect listening ability but the *kind* of experiences a listener has engaged in.

I.1.13 Organizational Ability. Although it is often assumed that organizational ability and listening are highly related, there is little evidence to support or refute this hypothesis. One study, however, did find that students who evidenced refined organizational skills tended to receive higher scores on both immediate and delayed recall tests than those who did not evidence such skills (Thompson, 1960). This particular study tends to confirm the hypothesis that persons who can organize materials mentally tend to listen more effectively. However, it is dangerous to make broad inferences based on the results of a single investigation.

I.1.14 Reading Comprehension. Listening and reading obviously are interrelated communication skills. They are similar in that the receiver relies on his background experience and vocabulary to interpret stimuli presented through both oral or written channels. The primary difference between the two communication modes is the communication channel each employs. The physical demands also differ for each medium.

In general, the relationship between reading and listening may be summarized as follows: In situations where students can listen easily to material or cope with word symbols orally, they prefer listening to reading. In situations where the material to comprehend is difficult or the conditions for listening are not favorable, students prefer reading.

I.1.15 Speech Training. Some research has attempted to correlate listening effectiveness with the number of courses taken or extracurricular speech activities engaged in. The results suggest that speech training in high school often improves listening skills to a moderate degree. The relationship is not a high one. It also might be noted at this point that most speech courses tend to focus on transmission of messages rather than on message reception. Obviously, this is partly a result of a curriculum decision and is also a function of the nature of the subject matter for speech courses. It does seem to be inconsistent, when dealing with a communication skill, to focus only on one half of the communication act rather than on the entire communication process. Fortunately, there is an increasing trend in many high schools and colleges to initiate speech communication courses which include listening as well as speaking training.

I.2. ADDITIONAL VARIABLES RELATED
TO LISTENING TO A LESSER DEGREE

In addition to those variables just discussed, some investigations have suggested (but not definitely established) that the following four factors may relate to listening ability:

I.2.1 Recognition of Correct English Usage.

I.2.2. Ability to Make Inferences.

I.2.3 Ability to Listen for Main Ideas.

I.2.4 Susceptibility to Distractions.

II. Speaker Qualities

II.1 Rate of Speaking.   Rate of speaking is another area of research with conflicting results concerning its influence on listening. One investigation indicated there is little effect on comprehension when a communicator speaks between the rate of 125 and 250 words per minute (Nelson, 1948). Another study concluded that an optimal speaking rate for comprehension is between 125 and 160 words per minute (Goodman-Malamuth, 1956). Still other investigations report different optimal speaking rates. Possible explanations for the conflicting findings may be differences in message content, academic level of the listener, length of the message, and conditions under which listening occurred. It would appear that for short time periods, most listeners can adapt to a very rapid rate of speaking (perhaps 400 words per minute or over) but for longer time periods the speech rate approximating 135-175 words per minute is best for most listeners.

II.2 Fluency of the Speaker. Though little research in this area has been conducted thus far, it appears that the more fluent the speaker—that is, the fewer vocalized pauses ("uh," "and-uh") and digressions he exhibits—the more listenable is his message. Of course, additional research needs to be conducted before fluency can be shown to be highly related to listening comprehension.

II.3 Visibility of the Speaker. Some research indicates that listening improves when the speaker is visible. This appears reasonable since much meaning is transmitted via nonverbal communication. For example, through facial expression, a speaker not only can add interest to his message but also can change the meaning of his words. Therefore, when a listener can see a speaker he usually can gain more meaning from the message as well as benefit from the interest that bodily movements and facial expressions provide.

II.4 Who the Speaker Is. Considerable research has been conducted in the area of credibility to examine the effects of the speaker's "image," personality, perceived status, etc. on his persuasiveness. There is little research to indicate whether or not a person will be listened to because of who he is. However, from the research that has been conducted, we may infer that the more credibility a speaker possesses, the more respect he will command and, consequently, the more people will listen to him.

II.5 How Well the Speaker Is Liked. This variable relates to speaker credibility discussed above. Research is conclusive that the more a listener likes a speaker, the more he will pay attention to the speaker.

11.6 The Speaker's Use of Gestures. This area of research also was alluded to previously. The research regarding this variable indicates that the more gestures a speaker uses the more information listeners will comprehend. Conversely, the fewer gestures a speaker uses the less information listeners will comprehend.

II.7 Audibility of the Speaker. The research findings in this area parallel logical inferences you might make. It suggests that speaker audibility directly affects listening ability. However, given an adequate audibility level, increasing volume further does not appear to increase listening ability.

III. The Message

III.1 Emotional Appeals. Considerable research has been conducted examining the effects of emotional appeals in messages on listening comprehension. One investigation (Carlton, 1954) demonstrated that a listener's personal values may influence his ability to comprehend words and ideas. Carlton discovered that people comprehended more words when the value structures they possessed were compatible with those in the message they heard. Additional research suggests that the *intensity* of the appeal is perhaps a more important factor. Research suggests that those who are strongly opposed to a given appeal will tend to listen more carefully to it than those who do not feel strongly about it. Early writers concerning listening suggested that emotion-rousing words and emotional points tend to interfere with comprehension. However, there is little empirical research to substantiate this hypothesis. Perhaps research would indicate that emotionally laden messages tend to make the listener pay more attention to the words themselves than to their meaning.

III.2 High Quality Materials. Although little research has been conducted involving this variable, the research published to date shows a slight indication that people listen more carefully to material which they regard highly. Conversely, they listen less carefully to material which they perceive to be of low quality. However, operational definitions of "quality" differ among individuals and therefore this variable is highly subjective.

IV. Environment

Here it should first be emphasized that most listening theorists suggest that good listeners do not let environment inhibit their listening ability. However, some research has been conducted to indicate that some environmental factors do tend to affect listening ability. It would be assumed, therefore, that people who let the communication environment interfere with their listening comprehension are not among the most proficient listeners.

IV.1. Room Ventilation and Temperature. It may be hypothesized that a room that is well ventilated and that has a temperature within the range of comfort is more conducive to listening than one that is too hot or too cold. The limited research to date supports this hypothesis.

IV.2 Use of Only One Language at Home. Listeners who are reared in an environment where more than one language is spoken usually have more difficulty in comprehending than listeners from a home where one language is spoken. The reason for this appears obvious. The problem of assimilating language symbols is directly related to listening. In early years the confusion arising from having two different codes to internalize, store, and analyze tends to inhibit all communication skills to some extent.

IV.3 Being an Only Child. Research has indicated that listeners who are only children tend to comprehend better than those who are members of larger families. Reasons for this finding are numerous. For example, only children are used to being listened to and are used to listening with little external interference. In an environment where more than one sibling is present there often are a large number of messages concurrently transmitted among children and parents of which many are of little importance. Consequently, the child in this environment learns to screen out certain messages. He also becomes accustomed to not always being listened to and is not reinforced for being a good listener himself.

IV.4 Seating Arrangement. Several investigations have examined the effect of sitting close together or far apart on listening comprehension and attitude change. The general results tend to indicate that the closer people sit to each other the more likely they are to listen carefully, whereas the further apart they are (i.e., the less they perceive themselves to be an integral part of the group) the less likely they are to listen effectively. An investigation conducted by the author with elementary school children found that sitting in a semicircle (as opposed to the general "block" classroom seating arrangement) tended to increase not only listening comprehension but verbal output as well.

V. Variables Not Related to Listening

As might be expected, some of the research involving variables hypothesized to relate to listening has not supported such relationships. However, since the scope of the research is limited and since a study reporting no significant findings does not necessarily prove that no relationship exists, it is probably best to view the following variables in light of your own experience and observations and ask yourself if they appear to be related to listening comprehension.

The following variables have, to date, not been found to relate to listening ability:

V.1 Optimism of Listener.

V.2 Social Ease of the Listener.

V.3 Listener Self-Satisfaction.

V.4 Economic Attitudes of the Listener.

V.5 General State of the Listener's Health.

V.6 Distance of the Listener from the Speaker.

V.7 Worries of the Listener about Personal Matters.

V.8 Ability in Note Taking.

V.9 Listener's Self-Concept.

V.10 Prior Interest in the Subject by the Listener.

Summary

In an attempt to isolate variables which contribute to effective listening, researchers have conducted numerous investigations. Many investigations have produced conflicting findings, and several explanations for differences among studies have been obvious. Some reasons for conflicting findings are: different content in messages among studies, different message lengths, different age and academic levels of students, different criterion variables (measuring instruments), and different operational definitions of both listening and criterion variables. Although little of the research cited in this chapter is "conclusive," the following variables appear to be related, at least moderately, to listening effectiveness:

I.   Listener characteristics, experiences, and abilities
I.1   Variables found to relate to listening skills to a moderate or high degree
I.1.1   Sex
I.1.2   Age
I.1.3   Personality characteristics
I.1.4   Motivation and curiosity
I.1.5   Interest and attitudes
I.1.6   Binaural hearing
I.1.7   Listener fatigue
I.1.8   Intelligence
I.1.9   Scholastic aptitude and achievement in high school
I.1.10 Verbal ability
I.1.11 Vocabulary size
I.1.12 Experience in listening
I.1.13 Organizational ability
I.1.14 Reading comprehension
I.1.15 Speech training

I.2   Additional variables related to listening to a lesser degree
I.2.1   Recognition of correct English usage
I.2.2   Ability to make inferences
I.2.3   Ability to listen for main ideas
I.2.4   Susceptibility to distractions

II.   Speaker qualities
II.1   Rate of speaking
II.2   Fluency of the speaker
II.3   Visibility of the speaker
II.4   Who the speaker is
II.5   How well the speaker is liked
II.6   The speaker's use of gestures
II.7   Audibility of the speaker

III.   The message
III.1   Emotional appeals
III.2   High quality material

IV.   Environment
IV.1   Room ventilation and temperature
IV.2   Use of only one language at home
IV.3   Being an only child
IV.4   Seating arrangement

V.   Variables which have, to date, not been shown to relate significantly to listening effectiveness
V.1   Optimism of listener
V.2   Social ease of the listener
V.3   Listener self-satisfaction
V.4   Economic attitudes of the listener
V.5   General state of the listener's health
V.6   Distance of the listener from the speaker
V.7   Worries of the listener about personal matters
V.8   Ability in note taking
V.9   Listener's self-concept
V.10   Prior interest in the subject matter by the listener

QUESTIONS FOR DISCUSSION

1. *What reasons, other than those mentioned in this chapter, can cause conflicting results to be obtained among similar experiments?*

2. *Which of the variables in this chapter that are noted to relate at least moderately to listening were surprising to you?*

3. *Which of the variables would you have intuitively thought to be related to listening effectiveness?*

4. *Of the variables noted which were* not *found to relate to listening effectiveness, which would you have assumed intuitively to relate to listening?*

5. *What dangers must one be aware of when applying the findings of experimental and descriptive research?*

6. *What applications to your own listening behavior can you make, on the basis of the research reported in this chapter?*

7. *What instances (or hypothetical situations) might tend to reverse the results of the investigations reported in this chapter?*

*Selected References for Chapter 3**

I.1.1 Caffrey *(1955)*; Paulson *(1952)*; Kramar and Lewis *(1951)*; Green *(1958)*; Brandon *(1956)*.

I.1.2 Brown *(1959)*.

I.1.3 Stromer *(1955)*; Sullivan, Jr. *(1946)*; Haberland *(1959)*; Prince *(1948)*.

I.1.4 Stephens *(1951)*; Irvin *(1953)*; Stromer *(1952)*; Nichols and Lewis *(1954)*.

I.1.5 Heath *(1951)*; Cartier *(1952)*; Vernon *(1950)*; Knower, Phillips, and Kroeppel *(1945)*.

I.1.6 Taylor *(1964)*.

I.1.7 Wiksell *(1946)*; Sorenson *(1948)*; Widener *(1950)*.

I.1.8 Erickson *(1954)*; Greene *(1928)*; Goldstein *(1940)*; Larson and Feder *(1946)*.

I.1.9 Brown and Carlsen *(1955)*; Green *(1958)*; Blewett *(1951)*; Nichols *(1948)*.

I.1.10 Hall *(1954)*; Crook *(1957)*; Kramar *(1955)*; Haberland *(1959)*; Krueger *(1950)*.

I.1.11 Park *(1945)*; Erickson *(1954)*; Anderson and Fairbanks *(1937)*; Nicholson *(1947)*.

I.1.12 Nichols *(1948)*; Tyler *(1946)*; Crawford *(1925)*; Crawler *(1938)*.

I.1.13 Thompson, Jr. *(1960)*; Adams *(1947)*; Schneider *(1950)*; Heilman *(1952)*.

I.1.14 Taylor *(1964)*.

I.1.15 Nichols *(1948)*.

I.2.1 through I.2.4 Nichols *(1948)*.

II.1 Goodman-Malamuth II *(1956)*; Nelson *(1948)*.

II.2 Utzinger *(1952)*.

---

* References after each identifying number refer to the section corresponding to that number in this chapter.

II.3 Gauger *(1951)*.

II.4 Paulson *(1952)*.

II.5 Haiman *(1949)*.

II.6 Haiman *(1949)*.

II.7 Nichols *(1948)*.

III.1 Carlton *(1954)*; Edwards *(1941)*; Berlo and Gulley *(1957)*; Matthews *(1947)*; Hovland, Janis, and Kelley *(1953)*.

III.2 Beighley *(1952)*.

IV.1 Nichols *(1948)*.

IV.2 Nichols *(1948)*.

IV.3 Nichols *(1948)*.

IV.4 Furbay *(1965)*.

V.1 through V.10 Petrie *(1961)*; Nichols *(1948)*.

IDENTIFYING
YOUR
LISTENING PROBLEMS

Objectives for Chapter 4

Upon completion of this chapter, you should be able to:

A. *Content Objectives*

(1) Identify, orally or in writing, three types of inner conflicts which can inhibit listening effectiveness.

(2) Specify, in writing, at least ten undesirable listening behaviors (or habits) which have been identified.

B. *Action Objectives*

(1) Identify undesirable listening behaviors (or habits) as they are evidenced.

(2) Modify or correct the undesirable listening behaviors identified in the above objective by (a) being sensitive to their occurrence and (b) making a conscious effort to engage in active listening when the undesirable behavior is isolated.

Problems are a paradox. Many people place problems and the weather in the same category. They talk a lot about their problems, but do nothing to solve them. Other people try to pretend outwardly that they have no problems—yet if you analyze their conversation, it reflects deep anxieties and concerns. This chapter is concerned with a particular type of problem which many people have acquired—a problem of practicing ineffective listening behaviors. These listening problems are different from other problems, for you may not even recognize that you have them. As you read each section of this chapter ask yourself "Is this a problem that I have in listening?" At the end of the chapter there is a summary and checklist of listening problems which can help you assess your own listening behavior and determine if you are guilty of any bad listening habits.

Before discussing some specific listening problems which serve as barriers to effective listening, we should point out some factors that tend to inhibit effective listening. These factors relate to the general mental state of the listener.

The first factor that can inhibit active listening is *inner conflict*. People who have problems of a personal or academic nature tend to devote considerable mental energy attempting to analyze their problems. This mental deliberation, in turn, often interferes with listening. The second factor, similar to inner conflict, is *general anxiety*. Such anxieties may be so generalized that it is difficult to verbalize their exact nature. Some inner conflicts may stimulate or increase general anxieties. Examples of situations which contribute to increased anxieties include: religious convictions which run counter to the norms of a group you want to join; fear of failure in a certain area such as school, social acceptance, or job; and personal problems with parents or a friend. Regardless of the cause of anxieties, when they demand a major proportion of conscious thought time they significantly decrease a listener's effectiveness. A third inhibitor of listening, *closed-mindedness*, will be discussed later at some length. It is difficult to analyze our own patterns of behavior to determine whether or not we are closed-minded. Many students pride themselves on being open-minded but are only open minded on a selective basis. In other words, they are open-minded about issues that coincide with their personal biases, but they may be closed-minded with regard to issues with which they do not identify. If you suspect you may be closed-minded in certain areas, try to examine critically your opinions, attitudes, and beliefs. If you find you have a tendency to be closed-minded as a listener, try to stretch your tolerance of other views. It is almost impossible to be a critical listener if you are closed-minded. One other general variable which no doubt contributes significantly to listening breakdowns is the tendency to try to do *too many things at the same time*. Although some students can study effectively while simultaneously listening to the stereo, watching TV, and eating a snack—most do not have sufficient perceptual skills to assimilate all of these stimuli in a meaningful and orderly manner. Similarly, listening usually demands full-time attention and perception. It is difficult to concentrate on receiving and interpreting a message if you are doing other things requiring some concentration at the same time. If you can set aside (mentally or physically) other tasks while you listen, your listening will be improved and you will not be tempted to engage in many of the bad listening habits which are discussed below.

Some Common Listening Problems

Having reviewed some of the mental conditions which can inhibit listening, let us now examine several specific problems which are inhibitors of effective listening.* In examining the following listening habits, first attempt to recall having observed others engaged in the habit. It often is easier to identify undesirable traits in others than to identify them in oneself. If you can recognize the behavior in someone else, the next step—a critical examination of your own listening behavior—will be more effective and, perhaps, less painful. It is comforting to know that others have problems similar to yours. It should be noted that, in many instances, several of these bad listening habits may be practiced simultaneously.

✓ (1) *Viewing a Topic as Uninteresting.* Most of us have been forced to enroll in at least one class in school because it was a "required" course, or because our advisor strongly recommended it. It may have been Chemistry, Spanish, Art, Speech, or one of a dozen courses which, although enjoyed by some other people, did not interest you at all. Do you remember how you behaved as a listener

---

* Several of the listening problems which follow were derived, with some adaptation, from Nichols and Stevens (1957).

in that class? Chances are if you succeeded in forcing yourself to listen through the first part of the course, your interest increased, at least minimally, and you did better in the course than you would have predicted. However, if you "turned off" the instructor early in the course, chances are that your previous perception about the uninteresting nature of the subject matter was reinforced, and that you did not excel in the course.

The key issue in discussing this listening problem is *efficiency* of your time and energy. Given that time is probably your most precious commodity (granted, money may run a close second), if you are forced by circumstances beyond your control to spend time in a communication situation where you can listen actively or passively, it seems reasonable that you try to make the best use of your time. Of course, you may argue that mentally "blocking out" the speaker's message so you can think about more important matters is a better use of your time than attentive listening. In some cases this may be true. However, since you happen to be in the situation anyway, it is possible you might learn something interesting or useful for future reference. With a little creative mental effort you can think of several applications a topic might have. Thus, although a subject may appear uninteresting at the outset, it is still possible to glean value through active listening. Be careful of mentally dismissing potential listening situations by prematurely calling topics uninteresting.

(2) *Criticizing a Speaker's Delivery Instead of His Message.* Students of speech and communication become sensitive to aspects of a speaker's delivery quite early in their education and experience —e.g., eye contact, voice quality, rate of speaking, volume. These elements are important to analyze from a communicator's point of view; speakers should be aware that aspects of delivery may negatively or positively affect untrained listeners. However, from the other point of view, the listener should try to overlook or repress negative aspects of the speaker's delivery which might interfere with the message. There are several ways to do this. You will have to discover which works best for you. The central concern in any approach should be to disregard negative or novel elements in the speaker's delivery or physical appearance.

(3) *Getting Overstimulated or Emotionally Involved.* This common listening problem is created when listeners are ego-involved with regard to the subject that a speaker is discussing. For example,

a member of Alpha Beta Kappa Sorority hears a speaker mention that ABK has the ugliest girls on campus. It is very probable, unless she is a good listener, that she will react emotionally to the remainder of the speaker's message. This emotional involvement may distort or interfere with her acquisition of important information which followed. In other words, it may cause an emotional "deaf" spot. In Chapter 5 some ways to control this tendency to become emotionally involved in what the speaker says will be discussed.

 ✓ (4) *Listening Only for Facts.* Students become conditioned early in their educational career to take notes in order to pass examinations. This conditioning process creates a type of listener who listens primarily for factual information that can be recorded on paper (to be reviewed and learned later). Obviously, there are times when it is imperative to listen exclusively for facts (e.g., when the commander on the battlefield issues the orders for the day's assault on an enemy stronghold). Listening only for facts is a dangerous listening habit only in selected instances. The major problem promoted by this practice is a tendency to avoid critical analysis and evaluation of the message while listening. In addition, if a message is rich with symbolism or multiple interpretations, the practice of listening primarily for facts may produce a distorted version of the message.

Analyze the communication setting, and determine the nature of the message. If facts are important, listen for them. If it is more important to interpret and analyze the message, do not listen for facts—begin evaluating.

(5) *Preparing to Answer Questions or Points Before Fully Understanding Them.* All of us have done this at some time or another. We think we know what the speaker is going to say and begin formulating mental or oral questions with regard to the projected message, or perhaps a great "comeback." This habit, at times, can make listeners appear foolish, rude, or not very bright. Be careful that you do not mentally jump so far ahead of the speaker, and begin to answer questions you think he is going to ask, that you miss part of his message. This caution will not only save you possible embarrassment but also can help you to obtain deeper meanings from the speaker's message.

 ✓ (6) *Wasting the Advantages of Thought Speed Over Speech Speed.* This problem is closely related to (5) above. We can think at a rate of over 400 words a minute; but speakers rarely talk at a rate of over 200 words a minute. This thought-speed–speech-speed differential must be taken into consideration, otherwise the listener's mind may run ahead of the speaker. In problem (5) this differential allowed the speaker to jump ahead and formulate an answer to a question that was never asked. The same problem relates to other areas of listening. Any listening habits that tend to distract the listener allow him to become mentally removed from what the speaker is saying. Constructive or destructive use of the time-rate differential often makes the difference between good and bad listeners. Some solutions to this problem will be presented in the next chapter.

(7) *Trying to Outline Everything.* This, again, is a habit which students often acquire. Many students try to outline everything beginning with Roman numerals, then going to capital letters, then Arabic numbers, small letters, and so forth. This tendency to organize is sometimes desirable, except when the speaker has a different organizational pattern, or no organizational pattern at all. The point is, be careful when you outline that you do not impose your own organizational plan on that of the speaker. If you do superimpose an outline on the speaker's message, it is possible that your notes will be misleading and cause problems later on. A positive suggestion is in order at this point. Rather than attempting to outline the message point by point, listen for a few minutes, and then jot down key ideas and concepts. Search the message mentally for the important points, and try to avoid getting caught up in extended examples.

(8) *Tolerating or Failing to Adjust to Distractions.* We tend to think of elementary school children as prone to disrupt classroom communication by such behavior as putting thumb tacks on chairs, throwing spit balls, paper wads, or chalk, and shooting rubber bands. However, students at all levels may cause, or at least tolerate, distractions in the classroom. Of course, there are occasional instances when you cannot control environmental distractions. Some examples are soft music being played in the background, noise, movement in the background, or similar physical distractions. College dormitories are prime examples of environments where numerous distractions are often present. Failure to adjust to, or compensate for, such distractions is a common listening problem. If you cannot modify the external environmental conditions, you must modify your own in-

ternal listening behavior in order to fully assimilate the message the speaker transmits.

(9) *Faking Attention.* A conservative gambler probably would bet a sizable amount that this practice has been tried at least once by every student in the nation's educational system today. There are times during which certain thoughts race through your mind, which are so interesting or so important that you cannot force yourself to listen to the speaker. Therefore, because of fear of punishment or embarrassment you pretend you are listening via your facial expression, eye contact, and perhaps an occasional nodding of your head. You hope that the speaker is not aware you are not listening to what he says. Occasionally, as suggested previously, this habit may be necessary (also see Chapter 5). At least the habit serves to reinforce the speaker, even though the rewards are not sincere. However, the problem arises when it becomes a *real* habit—that is, a conditioned response of which you are not consciously aware. If you often find yourself not remembering what the speaker has said, check yourself to see if you have been practicing this negative listening habit.

(10) *Listening Only to What is Easy to Understand.* This problem can be phrased very simply: listeners often tend to avoid difficult listening. This habit is similar to the habit of calling a subject uninteresting prematurely. Again, because of demands on your mental energy, you may tend to ignore or avoid what the speaker has to say. This tendency may cause problems in school, because you often need to listen when you are not motivated. If you find you frequently tend to avoid difficult listening, try to modify your behavior.

(11) *Allowing Emotionally Laden Words to Interfere with Listening.* This bad habit is similar to (3). However, in this particular instance, listeners react to specific words rather than the general idea expressed in the message. Such words as "pig," "mother," "Communist," and the like, tend to have emotional connotations built into them. Regardless of their context, such words often trigger what are called "signal reactions"—that is, you react to the *words* and not their intended meanings. Ways to overcome overreactions to emotionally laden words are discussed in the next chapter.

(12) *Permitting Personal Prejudices or Deep-Seated Convictions to Impair Comprehension and Understanding.* This bad habit

is probably a sub-classification of closed-mindedness. It exists when positions listeners hold dear are threatened or when listeners find themselves in situations in which they are strongly ego-involved. This is a difficult problem to overcome, since it is a deep-seated, fully conditioned one and is usually a function of general personality structure. However, if you are aware you have certain biases or convictions, you can at least become sensitive to them and attempt to moderate your reactions when such topics are discussed.

The above dozen listening problems are not exhaustive or mutually exclusive; they overlap in several instances. However, they are some of the more common bad habits of students and other listeners.

If you note problems similar to those discussed above which inhibit your listening ability, begin by becoming sensitive to them. Being aware of them when you are practicing them will serve as the first step toward avoiding them in the future. The result should make you a better listener.

The following section provides a partial summary of the above points and suggests some "checks" to help you analyze your own listening problems.

Identifying and Modifying Negative Listening Behaviors

The following set of questions is designed to help you determine if you have acquired one or more undesirable listening habits. Answer all questions as objectively as you can.

1. Do you often avoid getting into situations where you must listen to a speaker you feel will not be dynamic, personable, or stimulating?

2. Do you avoid listening to new and different topics which may challenge your intellectual capacity?

3. Do you yield easily to physical distractions in listening settings?

4. Do you become irritated by speakers' mannerisms or atypical behaviors?

5. Do you find your mind wandering frequently in difficult listening settings? In easy listening settings?

6. Do you become emotionally involved frequently with what a speaker is saying and let your emotions control your concentration and intellectual abilities?

7. Do you try to impose your own organizational pattern on others when listening to them?

8. Do you frequently fake attention?

If you answered any of the above questions "yes," you probably need to work on modifying your listening behavior. The next chapter presents some specific suggestions to modify undesirable listening habits.

Summary

The summary for this chapter is in the form of a checklist of listening problems. If you want to make a concerted effort to identify and modify those listening problems you might have, (1) make a copy of the following checklist; (2) attempt to identify as many of these habits as possible in other listeners (some of the habits are nonobservable and you will have to infer whether or not they are being practiced; however, practice in identifying the habits in others will, first, help you more clearly understand the nature of each habit, and second, help sensitize you to their presence in your own listening behavior); (3) keep a day-by-day record for several days each time you find yourself engaging in a negative listening habit; (4) each time you record the negative listening behavior, make a conscious effort to correct it at once; and (5) keep watching for and avoiding possible recurrences of the habit. Hopefully, if you concentrate on eliminating each habit soon after you identify its presence, your list will grow shorter and shorter through the week and your listening should improve accordingly.

CHECKLIST OF LISTENING PROBLEMS

Instructions: Make enough copies of this list for about a week. Use a separate sheet for each date. Begin by recording the date on the left. Then, using the problem abbreviations below, record problems you note in your own listening behavior on the appropriate lines. (Note: if you discover problems other than the ones discussed in the chapter, record them also.) Place a tally mark (e.g., IIII) in the *Identified* column, each time you note the presence of a particular problem during the day. Finally, place a check mark (√) in the right-hand column beside each habit you corrected successfully. Repeat the process on a separate sheet each successive day.

Date	Problems	Identified	Corrected
_____ 1.	_____	_____	_____
_____ 2.	_____	_____	_____
_____ 3.	_____	_____	_____
_____ 4.	_____	_____	_____
_____ 5.	_____	_____	_____
_____ 6.	_____	_____	_____

ABBREVIATIONS OF LISTENING PROBLEMS

Abbreviation	Problem
1. Uninteresting topic	Viewing a topic as uninteresting
2. Criticizing delivery	Criticizing a speaker's delivery instead of his message
3. Emotionally involved	Getting overstimulated or emotionally involved
4. Fact listening	Listening only for facts
5. Question answering	Preparing to answer questions or points before fully understanding them
6. Thought-speech speed	Wasting the advantages of thought speed over speech speed
7. Outlining everything	Trying to outline everything
8. Tolerating distractions	Tolerating or failing to adjust to distractions
9. Faking attention	Faking attention
10. Easy listening	Listening only to what is easy to understand
11. Emotional words	Allowing emotionally laden words to interfere with listening
12. Personal prejudice	Permitting personal prejudices or deep-seated convictions to impair comprehension and understanding

QUESTIONS FOR DISCUSSION

1. *How do people acquire undesirable listening behaviors?*

2. *Why do people tend to react emotionally to certain words and not to others?*

3. *What are ways to sensitize oneself to one's own listening problems?*

4. *What methods, other than the checklist provided in the chapter, might be employed to identify and modify undesirable listening behaviors?*

5. *How can one cope with inner tensions and anxieties during important listening situations?*

6. *How can listeners modify the listening setting in order to make their own listening more efficient and effective?*

7. *What should the role of the listener be in helping the speaker to make it easier for listening to take place?*

IMPROVING
YOUR
LISTENING BEHAVIOR

Objectives for Chapter 5

After you have completed this chapter you should be able to:

A. Content Objectives

(1) Identify, orally or in writing, at least ten suggestions to help improve your listening behavior.

(2) Specify three general questions to keep in mind while listening.

(3) Specify four mental processes which should be engaged in while listening.

(4) Specify four hints to improve note taking while listening.

(5) Specify at least three suggestions to help improve appreciative listening behaviors.

(6) Specify at least three ways in which a listener might modify the listening environment to enhance listening effectiveness.

B. Action Objectives

(1) Employ each of the suggestions for improving listening in your own listening behavior to determine those which can substantially increase your personal listening effectiveness.

(2) Employ the four mental processes specified in this chapter which should accompany successful listening during appropriate listening settings, in an effort to increase your listening skills.

(3) Employ the suggestions to improve note taking while listening in an effort to obtain a more accurate record of the message(s) to which you will be listening.

(4) Employ the suggestions to improve appreciative listening in your own listening behavior in an attempt to increase your enjoyment of listening.

(5) Modify listening environments, according to the suggestions specified in this chapter, in order to increase potential listening effectiveness by yourself and other listeners present.

Some "Common Sense" about Listening

This is a "how to do it" chapter. The suggestions that follow are gleaned from a variety of sources. They are based on personal experiences, observation, and descriptive and experimental research. However, most of them might be classified as "common sense" suggestions. They are ideas to which you probably will say to yourself upon reading, "Everybody knows that—that's just common sense." This observation will be entirely accurate. The only purpose for including such suggestions in this text at all is that often we tend to forget them or neglect to utilize them. If this chapter is to achieve its objectives, especially the action objectives, which are the more important ones, you must do more than merely read the suggestions —you must actively attempt to incorporate them in your own listening behavior. In fact, the suggestions found here should serve primarily to stimulate thinking about the general process of listening improvement and help you discover additional common sense suggestions on your own, which relate directly to your personal listening behaviors. The relationship between reading these suggestions and implementing them is similar to the relationship between getting solutions and solving problems. It is relatively easy to discover a variety of solutions to any problem you may encounter. However, solving the problem by implementing the best solution(s) is quite a different matter. Just as a problem is not solved until the solutions are successfully implemented, listening improvement does not occur until suggestions are successfully implemented in actual listening settings. Review the suggestions included in this chapter, but most important, *apply* them to your own listening behavior.

Before the *specific* suggestions to improve your listening behavior are presented, two general suggestions to help you become a better listener should be emphasized. The first is simply to be constantly aware that listening is vital to communication. A review of Chapter 2 will demonstrate the relationship between listening and the total communication process. In fact, if you already have read this far, you probably already are sensitized to listening as an important process, and consequently already are beginning to be a better listener.

The second general suggestion is to review the bad listening habits presented in Chapter 4 and attempt to modify or correct those which you recognize in your own listening behavior. Many of the suggestions in this chapter are, in essence, the positive statement of some bad habits discussed in Chapter 4. After reviewing that chapter, examine the following list of specific suggestions and attempt to adapt those which relate to your own listening behavior.

Some Specific Suggestions for Listening Improvement

(1) **Be Mentally and Physically Prepared to Listen.** This suggestion may be obvious, but active listening involves being physically and mentally "in shape." We take for granted that athletes involved in active competition must prepare their minds and bodies for the sport in which they are engaged. However, few people view listening as an activity which demands being in condition. Your attention span is directly related to your physical and mental condition at a given moment. If you are tired, your capacity to listen actively and effectively is reduced.

(2) **Think About the Topic in Advance When Possible.** In the case of classroom lectures it is often possible to read ahead about the lecture topic and devote some conscious thought to the issues in advance. The same holds true, to a lesser extent, when you plan to attend a public speech or public discussion. You should try to provide an opportunity to review in your mind considerations regarding the topic about which you will be listening. This suggestion is based on learning research, which supports the contention that, if you are somewhat familiar with a topic before you attempt to learn more about it, your learning takes place more efficiently and is generally longer lasting.

(3) **Behave as You Think a Good Listener Should Behave.** Several desirable listening behaviors have already been specified in this text. A partial summary of desirable listening behaviors might include:

(a) Concentrating all of your physical and mental energy on listening (see (7) in this section).

(b) Avoiding interrupting the speaker when possible.

(c) Demonstrating interest and alertness.

(d) Seeking areas of agreement with the speaker when possible.

(e) Searching for meanings and avoiding arguing about words (see (10) in this section).

(f) Demonstrating patience because you understand that you can listen faster than the speaker can speak (see Chapter 4).

(g) Providing clear and unambiguous feedback to the speaker (see Chapter 7).

(h) Repressing the tendency to respond emotionally to what is said (see Chapter 4).

(i) Asking questions when you do not understand something.

(j) Withholding evaluation of the message until the speaker is finished—and you are sure you understand the message (see (11) (a) in this section).

Try to imitate those behaviors which lead to effective listening. In addition, observe other people who are good listeners and model your own behavior in listening settings after them. In this particular instance, imitation not only may be a sincere form of flattery, it also may help you become a better listener.

(4) **Determine the Personal Value of the Topic for You.** This suggestion is designed to make you a "selfish listener." It is based upon the assumption that initial motivation to listen may not be sufficient without some added active effort on your part to perceive what may be gained by listening to the message. Search for ways in which you can use the information. Look for potential economic benefits, personal satisfaction, or new interests and insights. In other words, strive to make listening to the topic appear vital or rewarding for you.

(5) **Listen for Main Points.** The key word in this suggestion is "main." Look for those points which, in your estimation, represent the primary theme of the message, that is, the central idea the speaker is trying to impart. It is impossible to remember everything a speaker says. Therefore, try to isolate major points and do not attempt to memorize all of the sub-points. This suggestion, if followed, should help you begin to quickly identify important elements in the speaker's message while screening out less important points.

(6) **Practice Listening to Difficult Expository Material.** This is, perhaps, more of an exercise than a suggestion; but it has been found that by applying good listening habits to difficult listening, listening under normal circumstances can be improved. This same principle applies to other areas of mental and physical improvement. For example, if you practice shooting a basketball into a hoop smaller than regulation size, theoretically it should be easier to make baskets in a hoop of normal size. If you find you are an effective listener in extremely difficult listening settings, it is very probable you will be even more effective when listening under normal conditions.

(7) **Concentrate—Do Not Let Your Thoughts Wander.** Listening is an activity which is usually performed at relatively high speeds. Speaking can be performed at a variety of speeds, most of them considerably lower than normal listening speeds.

The listener should be aware of the difference between the rate of speech and the rate of thinking and should use the time lag effectively rather than letting it destroy the listening process. Some specific suggestions can help the listener use this time lag constructively to enhance the listening process.

(a) *Identify the developmental techniques used by the speaker.* This means, look at examples used, order of arrangement, and the mechanics of the message itself in an attempt to determine how the message is constructed and how it combines a set of ideas into a coherent unit (or if it does not combine ideas into a coherent unit).

(b) *Review previous points.* Use the time lag to review in your mind the points the speaker has made already. This may help you learn the material more completely and reinforce ideas the speaker has made so you can relate them to other parts of his message.

(c) *Search for deeper meanings than you received upon hearing the message for the first time.* Some words may have secondary or connotative meanings which you did not identify at first. Search the message for words which may have hidden meanings and apply these new meanings to the rest of the speaker's message.

(d) *Anticipate what the speaker will say next.* This sort of second guessing could be a bad listening habit if the listener does not compare what the speaker actually says with what he anticipated was going to be said (see Chapter 4). However, this suggestion can be useful if you try to evaluate what has been said, predict what will be said, and compare the actual message transmitted with that which you predicted. This active mental activity also can help reinforce the speaker's ideas in your mind and keep your attention focused on the message.

Obviously, you cannot engage in all four of these mental activities simultaneously. If you were to try, you probably would completely lose track of the speaker's message. You need to decide initially which of the activities should prove most beneficial in a given listening setting. This decision should be based, in part, on your specific purpose for listening.

(8) **Build Your Vocabulary As Much As Possible.** This suggestion has been stressed by educators for several years. Comprehension is directly related to a listener's having meaningful associations for the word symbols. In other words, listeners must have a sufficiently developed vocabulary to understand most of what the speaker is saying. In some instances it may even be necessary to learn a "new" vocabulary before attempting to listen. In the classroom you may need to review a new set of definitions or terms, or learn some key words which will be used throughout the course, in order to understand what the teacher is saying. A foreign language course provides a good example of the need to have a sufficient vocabulary in order to understand what is happening in class. This is why most language courses begin by having students memorize certain words; new words are then gradually added as they are used in the daily lesson.

(9) **Be Flexible in Your Views.** As was mentioned in Chapter 4, do not be close-minded. Examine your own views. Make sure the views you hold that are inflexible are held for a very good reason; and try to keep in mind that there may be other, contradictory views which may have some merit even if you cannot give them total acceptance. If you approach all listening situations with an open mind, you can only profit.

(10) **Compensate for Emotion-Rousing Words.** Some words evoke "signal reactions" (i.e., reactions which are a function of habit or conditioning) as opposed to cognitive deliberation. We must be aware of those particular words which affect us emotionally—for example, "sex," "nigger," "teacher," and most "four-letter" words—

and attempt to compensate at the cognitive level for them. Following are some specific suggestions to help compensate for emotion-rousing words. (a) *Identify, prior to listening, those words that affect you emotionally.* This step simply involves making yourself aware of specific words which you know stimulate signal reactions. (b) *Attempt to analyze why the words affect you the way they do.* What past experiences or encounters have created for you unique meanings for certain words? (c) *Try to reduce their impact upon you by using a "defense" mechanism.* One which is popularly suggested to help avoid emotional reactions to certain words is called "rationalization." Rationalization involves attempting to convince yourself that the word really is not such a bad word or it does not have any real referent. Another technique is to repress certain meanings of emotionally laden words and substitute new meanings. No matter what defense mechanisms you use, try to eliminate, insofar as possible, a conditioned or signal reaction to a word. Try to determine objectively what meaning the word holds for the speaker.

(11) **Compensate for Main Ideas to Which You React Emotionally.** This is similar to (10) in that there also are certain trains of thought, main points, or ideas to which we may react emotionally. For example, a listener may react very emotionally when the topic of compulsory arbitration in unions is discussed, because he is a long-standing union member. Students may react emotionally when the topic of grades is discussed, and so forth.

When you hear an issue being discussed to which you have an apparent emotional reaction, there are several suggestions which may help you compensate for your initial bias.

(a) *Defer judgment.* This is a principle suggested by Osborn (1962) in his text *Applied Imagination.* He suggests that in order to be a creative thinker, problem solver, or listener you must learn to withhold evaluation of ideas until you have listened to everything the speaker has to say. This suggestion often is difficult to employ because of prior experiences, positive or negative, that you may have had with certain ideas. However, if you can successfully employ the principle of deferred judgment you will become a more effective and appreciated listener.

(b) *Empathize.* This involves taking the speaker's point of view while you listen, and trying to discover why he says what he says. In essence, identify with the speaker, search for his reasons, views, and arguments which differ from your own but which, from his point of view, may nevertheless hold some validity.

(c) *Place your own personal feelings in perspective.* Try to realize that your past experiences, including your cultural and educational background, have molded you into a unique human being. As a result, you hold certain views which may be different from the views that others hold. Nevertheless, you must evaluate your own perceptions and feelings in light of those the speaker is trying to communicate. If you can critically evaluate your own views and feelings, you may be able to discover how they relate to or differ from those of the speaker.

Keep These Points in Mind When You Listen

The previous eleven suggestions relate to specific aspects of listening improvement. Following are some questions you should constantly keep in mind in all listening settings. If you can answer all of them at the end of each listening experience, the probability is high that you have listened successfully.

(1) *What does the speaker really mean?* This question was implied earlier, but is important to ask at all listening levels. Since you hold different meanings for words than the speaker as a result of differing past experiences, you must search actively to discover what message the speaker really is trying to communicate through his word symbols.

(2) *Have some elements of the message been left out?* People often speak without paying careful attention to the way they use certain words. Similarly, they often take for granted that the listener will fill in missing information in the message. The omission of information may be intentional or it may be subconscious on the part of the speaker. Therefore, you, the listener, have to take the active role in finding out what elements the speaker may have left out, which might help clarify and add meaning to his message.

(3) *What are the bases for the speaker's evidence?* This question implies that you must evaluate critically the reasons why a speaker advocates certain points. Is his evidence based on firsthand observation (perhaps this class of data may be called "facts") or is it

based primarily on personal opinion? If on opinion, is the speaker an expert (thought to have a valued opinion on the subject) or are his opinions based on inferences or secondhand observations? Is the speaker's evidence consistent with what you may know? Is it based on careful study or cursory observation? All of these considerations contribute to the validity of the speaker's arguments. As you begin to search and evaluate the speaker's evidence, you become more critically aware of the quality and importance of his ideas.

Some Hints for Note Taking *

Closely related to the listening process is the process of taking notes. Note taking is employed frequently in classroom settings, but also may be exercised in other public speaking or semiformal listening situations. Below are several suggestions designed to improve your note taking ability.

(1) **Determine Whether or Not to Take Notes.** Notes may be useful in some settings, but unnecessary, and even distracting, in others. Your purpose for listening should determine whether or not you need to take notes. If you feel you may need to refer to the information at a future time, the notes probably are necessary. However, if the information is for immediate use (e.g., announcements about the day's schedule at a summer workshop), it may be more effective simply to listen carefully without taking notes. Your own ability to comprehend and retain information is a variable which also must be taken into account. If you have high concentration and retention abilities, you probably will need to take relatively few notes. However, if you have difficulty remembering information the day after it is presented, you probably should get out the notepad.

(2) **Decide What Type of Notes are Necessary.** There are at least three different types of notes which people may elect to take. They differ in purpose and specificity. These three common types are key words, partial outline, and complete outline.

(a) *Key words.* When you primarily want to remember some

---

* Some of the suggestions in this section are derived, with some adaptation, from Lewis and Nichols (1965).

specific points in the message, key word notes are probably the most efficient. For example, if you wanted to remember an entertaining story about a member of Students for a Democratic Society who attended a meeting of the John Birch Society by mistake, so you could retell it later, you might elect to write the key words, "SDS at Birch meeting," on your notepad. Key words are used to help provide cues for ideas which were presented during the listening setting. However, unless you can positively associate the meaning with the key words, they are not of value.

(b) *Partial Outline.* If you decide that there are several important elements you should remember in a message, it probably is desirable to take notes in partial outline form. The points in the message which seem important to you are noted rather completely and other points which you do not deem important are not recorded. For example, if you are auditing a class on statistics and your professor illustrates how to compute a mean, median, and mode, you may decide that you want to remember only how to compute the mode. Consequently, you record in your notes only that portion of the lecture that relates to your specific interest. The notes you take are complete, but they do not represent all of the message that was presented.

(c) *Complete Outline.* In many lecture classes it is important to record most of what is presented in class. This is because you often will be expected to remember specific information later on tests. In such classes, and in other settings where you may need to have a complete record of what was said, a complete set of notes in outline form is necessary.

The key is to determine in advance what form of notes you will need to take in a given listening setting, and then adapt your note taking accordingly. If you modify your note taking according to the demands of the situation, you will make most efficient and effective use of your energy.

(3) **Keep Notes Clear.** This involves not only using brief sentences and statements of ideas which are understandable after you have written them, but involves such technical details as not cluttering the page, not scribbling, and not writing side comments. Use the paper efficiently; do not crowd words together.

(4) **Keep Notes Brief.** This suggestion speaks for itself. The briefer your notes, the less time you will be spending writing. This means you also will be less likely to miss what the speaker says.

(5) Note As Quickly As Possible the Organizational Pattern (Or Lack of Pattern) of the Speaker. First, be aware of the fact that many speakers have no discernible organizational pattern. There is a tendency for some note takers to try to organize notes on the basis of their own organizational patterns rather than the speaker's (see Chapter 4). For example, you may prefer outlining with Roman numeral I, followed by A and B, 1 and 2, a and b, and so forth. However, if the speaker is simply talking in random fashion without much formal organization, artificially imposing an organizational pattern on his message may distort this message. Therefore, it is important to note quickly if the speaker is employing a formal organizational pattern and adapt your own note taking to his pattern.

(6) Review Your Notes Later. This suggestion is extremely important in a learning theory framework because by reviewing information frequently it is possible to retain information more permanently. Ideas that we hear once tend to be forgotten within 24 hours. Without some review they may be lost to us forever. Another reason for reviewing your notes soon after taking them is that you may remember some subtleties at that point which you might not remember when reading your notes at some future time.

Appreciative Listening Suggestions

The previous suggestions in this chapter refer primarily to critical and discriminative listening settings. The suggestions below are designed to improve appreciative listening behavior in social or informal settings.

1. *Determine what you enjoy listening to most.* This suggestion requires a self-analysis to discover those listening situations in which you find yourself most frequently involved by choice.

2. *Analyze why you enjoy these listening settings.* Determining the reasons why you enjoy particular situations may help you more fully understand your listening preferences.

3. *Compare your own likes in listening with those of others.* By comparing your own likes with those of others you can derive some social reinforcement for the types of listening you enjoy.

4. *Be curious.* Have an inquisitive mind about everything you hear. Try to be constantly creative and noncritical in the way you approach listening settings.

5. *Read and consult to learn more about those areas in which you enjoy listening.* Find out as much as you can about the subject (or music) to which you like to listen. Get more out of listening by being mentally prepared regarding the subject prior to engaging in listening.

An Ideal Environment for Listening

In some situations you may have control over the listening environment. The following suggestions may be helpful in structuring the environment for effective listening. Teachers generally have control over classroom listening environments; consequently, several of the specific suggestions that follow are derived from classroom listening.

(1) *Establish a comfortable, quiet, relaxed atmosphere in the room.* Listening is usually more successful when there are few physical distractions. It is possible to create an atmosphere that is so comfortable that the listener may become sleepy or drowsy. However, it is more probable that noise and other elements in the environment will distract the listener. These elements should be controlled. (2) *Make sure the audience senses a clear purpose for listening.* This may involve a brief explanation or preview on your part of what is ideally supposed to take place in the listening setting. The reason for this suggestion is obvious. When motivation is present (that is, perception of personal purpose), listening effectiveness is increased. (3) *Prepare the listeners for what they are about to hear.* This involves more than just providing them with a purpose for listening. It involves giving them some background in the content area of the message—e.g., define critical terms or provide a conceptual framework for the message. (4) *Break up long periods of listening with other activities.* How long a person can listen depends on many factors, such as his immediate physical condition, the air temperature, humidity, time of day, and so forth. For adult listeners a maximum time period for concentrated listening probably should be one hour, or less, if possible. If you are in control of a situation in which listening is to take place, you should intersperse other activities, hopefully involving physical action, so that the listeners can seek a diversion, become relaxed, and become mentally and physically prepared for the next listening session.

As was noted in Chapter 4, many bad listening habits often are practiced simultaneously. Similarly, many of the suggestions in this chapter for improving your listening effectiveness interrelate. For example, when you concentrate hard on what the speaker is saying, (7), you also are likely to be searching for main points, (5), and behaving like a good listener should behave, (3). Similarly, if you are truly flexible in your views, (9), you are likely to try not to let yourself become overstimulated by emotional words, (10), or ideas, (11).

In conclusion, the suggestions in this chapter are intended primarily to provide a basis for listening improvement.* They are by no means exhaustive, and all of them may not apply in every listening situation. The objectives of the chapter will have been realized if you have carefully examined each suggestion, applied it to your own personality and listening behavior, and assessed its usefulness. Remember, understanding concepts about listening without trying to improve your own listening behavior is of little value.

Summary

Sensitivity to listening problems is probably the most effective means of improving listening behavior. However, several "common sense" suggestions also can help interested listeners become more effective in a variety of listening settings. Among the suggestions to help improve listening are the following: (1) be physically and mentally prepared to listen; (2) think about the topic in advance when possible; (3) behave as good listeners should behave; (4) determine the personal value of the topic for you; (5) listen for main points; (6) practice listening to difficult expository material; (7) concentrate—do not let your thoughts wander; (8) build your vocabulary as much as possible; (9) be flexible in your views; (10) compensate for emotion-rousing words; (11) compensate for main ideas to which you react emotionally.

Some general questions to keep in mind while listening are: (1) What does the speaker really mean? (2) Have some elements of

---

* Appendix B includes several games, projects, and exercises which reinforce and supplement the suggestions for listening improvement presented in this chapter.

the message been left out? (3) What are the bases for the speaker's evidence?

Some hints for note taking include: (1) determine whether or not to take notes; (2) decide what type of notes are necessary; (3) keep notes clear; (4) keep notes brief; (5) note as quickly as possible the organizational pattern (or lack of pattern) of the speaker; (6) review your notes later.

The previous suggestions relate primarily to critical and discriminative listening settings. The following suggestions relate to appreciative listening: (1) determine what you enjoy listening to most; (2) analyze why you enjoy these listening settings; (3) compare your own likes in listening with those of others; (4) be curious; (5) read and consult to learn more about those areas in which you enjoy listening.

When listeners have an opportunity to modify the listening environment to enhance the probability of effective listening they should (1) establish a comfortable and quiet, relaxed atmosphere in the room (but not too comfortable), (2) make sure the audience senses a clear purpose for listening, (3) prepare listeners for what they are about to hear, and (4) break up long periods of listening with other activities.

QUESTIONS FOR DISCUSSION

1. *What are ways to become more sensitive to one's own listening behavior as a prerequisite to improving listening skills?*

2. *What are some ways, in addition to those included in this chapter, to help compensate for "signal reactions" to emotional words and ideas?*

3. *What modifications in the communication environment can listeners make while they are engaged in the listening process?*

4. *What modifications in the communication environment can listeners make before the communication process begins, in addition to those specified in this chapter?*

5. *Which of the listening suggestions included in this chapter appear hardest to implement successfully? Why?*

6. *Which of the listening suggestions included in this chapter appear easiest to implement successfully? Why?*

LISTENING TO BIASED COMMUNICATION

Objectives for Chapter 6

Upon completing this chapter you should be able to:

A. Content Objectives

(1) Describe, in writing, the natures of (a) rumors and (b) propaganda, including appropriate definitions and examples of each.

(2) Describe, in writing, Allport and Postman's law of rumor.

(3) Specify, orally or in writing, at least six ways in which rumors may be classified.

(4) Specify, orally or in writing, the three ways in which rumors tend to change when passed from person to person.

(5) Specify, orally or in writing, at least six generalizations about rumors which have been made on the basis of descriptive and experimental research.

(6) Specify, orally or in writing, at least four generalizations about rumors which have been made on the basis of case studies and observation.

(7) Specify, in writing, at least four suggestions to help analyze and evaluate rumors.

(8) Specify, in writing, at least eight propaganda devices.

B. Action Objectives

(1) Successfully identify and assess the validity of actual rumors.

(2) Successfully identify and analyze propagandistic messages.

(3) Inform others of ways to identify and assess both rumors and propaganda.

This chapter is about biased communication. The terms "rumor" and "propaganda" are used to describe two different types of biased communication. These two forms are interrelated and each places unique demands on the effective listener. A major difference between rumors and propaganda is that rumors may or may not be transmitted consciously—i.e., they may or may not be intended to impart a bias. On the other hand, propaganda is consciously developed and transmitted—i.e., intended to be biased communication by the originator of the message. Before we go any further, it should be pointed out that most, if not all, communication is biased to a certain extent. However, the nature or amount of bias, in most cases, is insufficient to alter the perceived credibility or effects of the message. For example, when you encourage your friend to buy the same make of car that you own, you no doubt are somewhat biased in your message. Even though your friend may be subconsciously aware that your message reflects your bias, it probably will not affect his reaction to your message. In other instances, however, a bias may be perceived as being malicious in intent. Such a perception, regardless of its validity, can totally destroy the impact of the message. Rumors and propaganda are defined here as biased communication because these are specialized types of communication in which bias, or perceived bias, is a primary defining characteristic. In many other types of communication, bias is a by-product, or secondary characteristic.

Examples of rumors are numerous. If you think about your interpersonal communication activities during the past week, it is highly probable that you can remember several rumors which you either heard or were instrumental in transmitting to others. They may have ranged from personal rumors about yourself or your friends to national rumors involving governmental policy and international relationships.

Examples of propaganda also are numerous but are not as easy to identify, at least by the layman. Most people impart a negative connotation to the term "propaganda." They may think of it primarily as being initiated by "Communist" or subversive elements in society. As will be noted later in the chapter, this is a limited and misleading perception of the nature and composition of propaganda. In fact, propaganda exists in most newspapers and magazines that you read everyday. There is nothing inherently bad about propaganda. It simply is a form of communication with a definite "built-in" bias. The motivating purpose behind the bias may be evaluated subjectively as either good or bad. However, this is not a criticism of propaganda but of how the message originator chooses to use it. (The same analogy holds true with propaganda as with any tool—the user may wield it wisely or foolishly, for good or for bad. For example, a knife may be used to help a man stay alive or to kill him.)

Propaganda probably is a somewhat outdated term. It is useful to classify certain kinds of messages as propaganda for purposes of discussion, but when you are forced to differentiate between these propagandistic messages and others, the distinctions are often not clear. In a sense, all propagandistic messages are persuasive messages. Some communication scholars would argue that *all* communication is persuasion—therefore, it could be argued logically that all communication is propagandistic in nature. Even though this argument might be valid, it is still useful to view propaganda in the generally accepted framework for purposes of discussion and analysis. For the sake of clarity, the natures of rumor and propaganda will be discussed independently.

Rumor *

One of the earliest definitions of rumor was offered by Allport and Postman (1947, p. ix). They defined rumor as "a specific (or topical) proposition for belief, passed along from person to person, usually by word of mouth, without secure standards of evidence being present." It is interesting to contrast this definition with that proposed by Shibutani (1966, p. 17): ". . . a recurrent form of communication through which men caught together in an ambiguous situation attempt to construct a meaningful interpretation of it by pooling their intellectual resources."

You will note that the first definition emphasizes the technical aspects of rumor transmission, that is, the fact that rumors usually are passed on verbally from one person to another. The second definition emphasizes the sociological aspects of rumor. It stresses the "pooling" of resources in an attempt to interpret ambiguous com-

* A substantial bibliography on rumor may be found in Shibutani (1966), pp. 227-55.

munication. Both definitions emphasize the element of ambiguity or the lack of sufficient information to ascertain the truth of the rumor. It is important, at this point, to remember that rumors are not necessarily false—most simply are ambiguous. It is the responsibility of the critical listener to ascertain the truth or falsity of the rumor. Generalizing from these definitions, it may be seen that rumors are biased, in many instances unintentionally. The bias may be amplified as the ambiguous statement is transmitted from one listener to another, then to another, and so on.

Unfortunately, most people, when they hear a rumor, tend to believe there is at least an element of truth in it. In fact, most people preface the transmission of a rumor by saying, "It's only a rumor, but—" $\times$. The implication inherent in the very act of transmitting a rumor is that there is a probability that some truth exists in it. Otherwise, why would it even be repeated? Research in the areas of persuasion and attitude change has suggested that people, after a period of time, tend to forget the source of a message they once heard, but often remember the content. When applied to rumors, this theory suggests that people often forget that the messages they heard were rumors, even though they were initially identified as such by the sender of the message. This is one reason why some statements which are, in essence, rumors often begin to be transmitted as "facts" after the third or fourth transmission of the message from one person to another. Research in organizational communication has demonstrated that qualifying statements tend to "drop out" when information is transmitted serially (from person to person).

A LAW OF RUMOR

As early as 1947, Allport and Postman formulated a "law" based upon their observation and research which attempted to predict the amount of rumor that could be in circulation under given conditions. Their law was expressed as follows: $(R \sim i \times a)$ (p. 33). They interpreted these symbols as follows: "The amount of rumor (R) in circulation will vary with the importance (i) of the subject to the individuals concerned *times* the ambiguity (a) of the evidence pertaining to the topic at issue" (p. 34). This would be a difficult law to test empirically, but the two variables which Allport and

Postman predict affect the amount of rumor allowed to be generated —subject importance and ambiguity of evidence—appear reasonable and important to keep in mind. Shibutani (1966, p. 57) expands upon this law to form a hypothesis relevant to social rumors. "If the demand for news in a public exceeds the supply made available through institutional channels, rumor construction is likely to occur." This statement demonstrates clearly one important characteristic of rumors. They tend to exist when the public feels a need for information or believes a problem exists which needs to be explained or solved.

CLASSIFICATION OF RUMORS

Listeners can gain considerable insight into the nature of rumors by examining the way in which psychologists and sociologists have classified rumors. Such classifications provide several operational definitions of rumors. Allport and Postman (1947) provide the following ways to classify rumors.

(1) *By speed or other temporal aspects of rumor.* Some rumors begin very slowly and pick up speed. Others arise almost "full blown." Such "instant" rumors usually evolve under crisis or other emergency situations. Other types of rumors tend to recur. They often appear to be disintegrating or losing momentum, but then reappear.

(2) *By the subject matter with which the rumor deals.* Wartime rumors tend to deal with such topics as: (a) horror, death, and disease; (b) general waste and lavish extravagance; (c) threats to security such as raids and invasions; and (d) alleged incompetencies in the way in which the war is being conducted. In non-wartime the content of rumor might be expected to deal with such issues as sex, politics, sickness, foreign relations, racial relations, minority groups, discrimination, and so forth. In addition, rumors from different regions of the country as well as from persons in different economic and social groups tend to focus on different topics and subject matters.

(3) *By the motives underlying the rumor.* In wartime most motives reflect hostility, fear, or desire. In non-wartime the motives of rumor initiators may be the same; however, the perception of motives by the listener may not be as easy. In "normal" times lis-

teners often tend to repress the notion that communicators may have unworthy motives. Thus the detection of rumors may be more difficult.

(4) *By the social effects of the rumor—be they beneficial, detrimental, or indifferent.* Some rumors (e.g., increased benefits for the aged under social security and medicare) tend to be wishful thinking on the part of those who might benefit from the rumor. Others (e.g., lowering of age for conscription into the armed services) reflect fear on the part of the listener. The effects of the rumor upon a certain segment of society can usually be inferred, if not directly measured. This category probably is one of the most useful in classifying rumors.

(5) *As local or widespread rumors.*

(6) *As new rumors or old.*

(7) *As plausible or nonplausible rumors.*

(8) *As rumors of long or short duration.*

CHANGES IN RUMORS

Allport and Postman (1947) determined that there were at least three recurring changes in rumors as they pass from person to person. These three effects are leveling, sharpening, and assimilation.

Leveling describes the tendency for rumors to become shorter, more concise, and more easily understandable to the listener. *Sharpening* refers to people's tendency to listen to what they want to listen to (the process of selective perception) and to retain only a limited number of details. *Assimilation* refers to the tendency for rumors to become internally more consistent as a function of people's adding elements which were initially missing, in order to make the rumors appear more plausible and cognitively reasonable.

The experiments conducted by Allport and Postman and others tend to confirm that these three effects of rumors are consistent in most types of rumors. Most of them may be explained in terms of human limitations, primarily with respect to memory and perception. The effects rumors may have on society or on individual listeners are primarily a function of the relationship between a particular rumor and its immediate audience. No generalized statement regarding effects can be made which covers all types of rumors and audiences. However, most people who have been affected in some way by rumors realize that rumors may have serious negative implications for interpersonal relationships and trust. Consequently, it is desirable to avoid transmission of rumors when possible and to keep all forms of communication on an objective and logical plane.

Some Generalizations from
Research and Observation
about Rumor °

There is a considerable body of experimental and descriptive research relevant to the process of rumor—most of it was conducted within the past three decades. On the basis of existing research the following generalizations seem tenable: (1) If people desire information, and it is not available through formal communication channels, rumors are likely to be conducted and transmitted. (2) The range over which a rumor is distributed depends upon, first, the number of persons available to receive and retransmit the rumor, and second, the geographic location of these people with reference to each other. The accessibility of communication channels also is a limiting factor in rumor distribution. (3) If people are only moderately concerned about obtaining information, their collective excitement is mild. Rumors which evolve in this environment are usually a product of critical deliberation. (4) When rumors are initiated through specific communication channels (e.g., public relations director of a large corporation), interaction is critical for their distribution. The content of this type of rumor tends to be consistent with what the public expects and desires. (5) If listeners desire information to a great extent, group excitement is generated and intensified. Consequently, the construction of rumors takes place as a result of spontaneous interaction among group members. Rumors constructed in this manner might be termed "extemporaneous rumors." (6) If group excitement is very great, rumors are constructed much more rapidly. The quantity of rumors generated is only limited by the availability of communication channels. (7) When people do not perceive a problem as pressing or important, the process of constructing rumors tends to slow down and eventually disappears. (8) In an ambiguous situation, even after rumors

° These generalizations are derived with some adaptation from Shibutani (1966).

have been tested for their truthfulness and results are provided, most people will hold strongly to those aspects of the rumor which support their own personal interests and beliefs. (9) The more emotional overtones accompanying a rumor, the more likely the rumor will be distorted in the transmission process and in retransmission.

The following are some additional generalizations which may be made about rumors on the basis of several case studies and observations: (1) Rumors usually are temporary in nature, that is, they involve elements in their content which are of current interest value or are specific and topical. (2) Rumors tend to run in cycles. Occasionally an old rumor will be revived by somebody who had not heard it before and will give it "new life" by initiating a second cycle. This second hearing of a rumor often adds credibility to it among people who heard it the first time, because at that time they probably were uncertain as to its truth. (3) The content of most rumors deals with either events or people. Movie stars, politicians, disasters, and personal weaknesses are among the most frequent subjects. (4) Immediate verification of a rumor is usually very difficult or impossible. This generalization is extremely critical, because it helps perpetuate a favorable climate in which rumors may thrive. (5) Initiators of rumors generally are not experts regarding the subject matter of the rumor. It is obvious that given a particular subject, experts are in a better position to assess the validity of a statement than laymen. Consequently, few rumors are initiated by people who are experts in that given field. It is more common for a layman to misquote an expert and thus start a rumor, or for a nonexpert to have insufficient evidence or information to evaluate a statement. Because few people are experts on many different subjects, the climate for rumors is very favorable and the communication environment is "rumor prone." Furthermore, because people often are busy, they do not have or want to take the time to verify rumor statements and, consequently, rumors are allowed to flourish.

WHAT CAN LISTENERS DO ABOUT RUMORS?

There are several things listeners can do to avoid being deceived or misinformed by rumors. A prerequisite for combatting the negative effects of rumors is to first identify a rumor as a rumor. There are several criteria which may be employed to determine whether or not a statement is a rumor. These criteria are similar to those suggested by Haney (1967) to help discriminate between statements of observation (fact) and statements of inference (rumor). In essence, a rumor is a statement based on an inference. Rumors are not statements of observation, by definition, because they are, at best, secondhand reports of another person's observation. Haney suggests that there are four general tests to help discriminate among statements of observation and statements of inference.

Statements of Observation	*Statements of Inference*
1. Can be made only *after* observation.	1. Can be made at any time.
2. Must be limited to what one has observed—must not go beyond. (I observed the man *wearing* the tie —his *buying* it, if he did so, was beyond my observation.)	2. Can go beyond observation— well beyond. We can infer to the limits of our imaginations.
3. Can be made only by the observer. (The observational statements of another are still my inferences, assuming that I have not observed what he has.)	3. Can be made by anyone.

These three requisites of observational statements are vital. You simply do not have a statement of observation if each of these criteria is not satisfied. A fourth pair of characteristics provides a helpful, but not an essential, contrast:

4. Statements of observation approach certainty.	4. Statements of inference involve only degrees of probability.

By equating observations and inferences with facts and rumors, it is possible to employ these criteria to help identify statements of rumor. Once a statement is identified as a rumor, there are several additional checks which may be employed to help discern its validity.

(1) *Check the source.* If a statement is about or attributed to another person who is available to you for consultation, ask the person if the rumor is true. Of course, if the information is of a personal nature this tactic may not be appropriate. However, when the direct approach is possible it can help stop malicious rumors and correct

distorted statements. The direct approach of checking with the source often is so obvious that it is taken for granted and probably is not employed with sufficient frequency.

(2) *Check with the transmitter, or "carrier," of the rumor to determine bases of information contained in the rumor.* Was the statement based on direct observation by the carrier? Was it second-hand—based on a reliable report by someone who did observe an event? Was it based on third or fourthhand reports? It is obvious that the more people a rumor passes through, the more likely it is to be distorted and the less probable it will be that it is completely true. The game of "rumor" (see Appendix B) demonstrates this aspect of rumor transmission.

(3) *Determine the consequences of the rumor for you and other people concerned if the rumor is true or false.* If the rumor is relatively inconsequential, it probably is not important to try very hard to determine its validity. In other words, if it does not affect the health or happiness of anyone, then perhaps the rumor can remain unverified with relatively little harm. However, if health or happiness are in jeopardy, for you or someone else, it obviously is important to continue searching for the factual basis of the rumor.

(4) *Try to assess what motives might have contributed to the rumor.* Were the motives of the person from whom you learned the rumor above reproach? Were the motives of the person who originated the rumor initially (if known) questionable? If there is no reason to suspect ulterior motives, it is more probable that the rumor contains some elements of truth which deserve further scrutiny. If ulterior motives are highly probable on the part of one or more persons responsible for transmitting the rumor, it is highly probable that some elements in the rumor may not be truthful. Keep in mind that even if motives are "pure," human communication breakdowns can occur, especially when a message is transmitted from person to person. People with the highest of motives still may confuse facts or invert information and unknowingly insert elements in the rumors.

(5) Given that you have reason to suspect that there are elements of truth in a rumor, the next step is both the most complicated and the most important. *Attempt to conduct systematic research to uncover evidence which will prove or disprove the critical elements in the rumor.* This procedure involves some knowledge of the "method of science." It is beyond the scope of this text to describe in full the method of science. However, several texts are available

which do so. (See Kaplan, 1964, Bormann, 1965, or Kerlinger, 1964.)

The scientific method encourages a systematic inquiry into the validity of hypotheses or observations. Sometimes the research simply involves going to the library and checking details in books or periodicals. At other times research involves interviewing people who would be in a position to know about critical elements in the rumor. Sometimes the research involves "undercover" investigations in which you must make several personal observations and then assess the reality or truth of the situation.

Do not forget that, even though you employ the scientific method to determine the facts in a given situation the results you obtain still only approach degrees of probability that your assessment of the statement or rumor is correct. You still must make some subjective inferences to make your final decision. When rumors have nonfactual bases—that is, when they involve assertions about personal characteristics or plans in the future—which are not immediately verifiable, the research procedures are considerably more difficult. It is then necessary to discover possible connections between the unknown elements in the rumor and those events which are known or may be inferred from past behaviors or observations. Identifying such connections between the known and the unknown can help in making qualified inferences about the truth of the rumor. In a case where you are predicting future outcomes, the truth of a rumor cannot be ascertained entirely until the predicted event actually occurs. However, you can make educated guesses in advance by trying to assess all the known facts and then making some thoughtful predictions based on this evidence.

It should be noted that some of the above suggestions also are useful in assessing propaganda. The following section describes the nature of propaganda and gives several additional suggestions to help deal with this type of biased communication.

Propaganda

At the beginning of this chapter a distinction was made between the two forms of biased communication: rumors may or may not be consciously designed, whereas, propaganda involves a *con-*

scious attempt to influence others through communication. The purpose, then, of propaganda is to convince somebody about something, usually about a controversial issue. The public usually identifies propaganda as "something recommended for the moment in relation to people's temporary or permanent demands, which involves their former experience or their opportunity to test the content of the recommendations immediately" (Dovring, 1950, p. 5). At this point it is important to reemphasize that propaganda may, in itself, be either good or bad, although the common tendency is to label all known propaganda as negative. Propaganda attacking racial discrimination, air and water pollution, disease, unequal housing standards, and so forth is generally considered desirable. The desirability is not lessened by the fact that appeals often are based on primarily emotional rather than intellectual factors. In fact, *all* messages that employ excessive emotional appeals in order to achieve a desired end may be termed propaganda messages. Thus, the question is not whether or not propaganda should be criticized or eliminated, but rather how its intent can be identified and analyzed. Until you can identify propaganda successfully you might tend to operate on the assumption that messages you receive are nonbiased. You may not be aware of hidden motives underlying messages or of the destructive impact of a message on others. One frequent characteristic of propaganda campaigns is an increase in the number and intensity of rumors circulating related to the content or intent of the propaganda. Rumors and propaganda are interrelated in this sense, because propaganda can thrive on rumors and vice versa.

Dovring (1959) suggests that "propaganda appeals to public interests in particular community values when controversial issues come up for discussion and decision. These appeals not only reveal the course of mass communication; they also invoke the communicator's strategy as to the public influence or understanding" (p. 123).*
In trying to further define some characteristics of propaganda it is important to remember that mass communication is the most common channel through which propaganda is transmitted. It is trans-

---

* It is important to emphasize that, although propaganda is generally identified with the mass media, it also may be initiated by single speakers, dyads (two-person groups), and small groups and organizations.

mitted through every conceivable medium from newspapers, magazines, and books, to billboards, public speaking, music (for example, protest songs), radio and television, and film. Propaganda may be received through all of the sensory receptors, including sight, sound, smell, and, perhaps even taste. Propaganda may even appear in the form of poetry or art.

IDENTIFYING PROPAGANDA

The first step in identifying a given message as propagandistic is to examine to whom the message is addressed. In public speeches, the speaker often will provide such clues as "brothers and sisters," "friends," "neighbors," or even "ladies and gentlemen." These addresses suggest a broad audience and not a specific sub-group within the audience. The speaker's introduction often reveals what might be termed a social framework for the message. Since messages often are not directed at someone specifically, the content of the message must be analyzed to see what specific members of the general public the message is trying to reach. Content analysis methods (see Chapter 7) have been developed which can help make this task systematic and even somewhat scientific. Although these methods may be cumbersome in some instances, a brief content analysis of general topics, ideas, and examples can yield much information about the intended receiver of the message and, perhaps, the speaker's real purpose in communicating.

When examining the purpose of a message in order to determine the presence of propaganda, perhaps the most important test is to determine whether the communicator or the general public will be served if the ideas proposed are implanted. If it appears that the suggested plan proposed in a message will benefit primarily the originator of the message or the group he represents (more than the public at large) the message may be identified clearly as propaganda.

Keep in mind, however, that even though a message may benefit the speaker, it is only reasonable that he would not be willing to expend time and energy communicating if he did not think his plan had value. Here, again, is the issue of separating good from bad propaganda. The fact that a message does happen to be biased does not necessarily mean that the results from accepting it would be bad. Likewise, even though a propagandistic message may benefit the originator of a message, it may benefit other members of society as well.

During World War II several agencies attempted to make stringent tests which would measure the presence or absence of propaganda in a message. These tests were supposedly designed to help protect the free world from biased communications. Several of these tests are listed below. It is beyond the scope of this text to explain them in detail. However, the interested reader should consult Dovring (1959), pp. 121-22, for a further explanation of them.

1. *Avowal test.* This test attempted to indicate how a message identified itself with one or the other side of a given controversy.

2. *Parallel test.* This test was designed to measure the outcome of a comparison between the themes of a known propaganda channel and what might be termed "doubtful" messages at home.

3. *Consistency test.* This test tended to disclose agreement with declared propaganda aims of a controversial party.

4. *Presentation test.* This test aimed at solving the important problems of maintaining balance and dealing with controversial issues and sources of information.

5. *Source test.* This test had the same objective as the presentation test.

6. *Concealed source test.* This was a further attempt at identifying sources of information.

7. *Distinctiveness test.* This tested given parties' use of a particular vocabulary in order to identify particular affiliations within or across parties.

8. *Distortion test.* This test dealt with omissions, additions, and over or underemphasis, as well as modifications of a common topic in a favorable or unfavorable position.

In non-wartime conditions, such tests are perhaps not as useful as during a war and may not apply to many of the types of propaganda that exist today. However, there is room for experimentation with new means to identify whether or not messages contain propaganda and to cope with such messages, measure them, and draw logical conclusions from them. We should be reluctant to base decisions about *any* messages solely on the basis of emotional appeals.*

PROPAGANDA DEVICES

In 1930 the Institute for Propaganda Analysis embarked on a major campaign to help inform the American public about propaganda devices and techniques. The following propaganda devices were among those identified by the Institute in 1938: (1) half truths, (2) card stacking, (3) hasty generalizations, (4) glittering generalities, (5) name calling, (6) labeling, (7) transfer, (8) testimonials, (9) plain folks, (10) dynamite words, (11) bandwagon.

Most of these propaganda devices are self-explanatory, but a few brief comments about each should help clarify those which might be unclear. (1) *Half truths* involve telling only part of the story deliberately when the full story is known to the message originator. Deliberate elimination of basic elements in the message is really a form of lying—by omission rather than comission. (2) The second device, *card stacking*, is another type of "lie" because it involves presenting only one side of an argument and withholding information which might refute the position being advocated. Card stacking can be a serious threat to the listener because it involves the manipulation of evidence in order to support positions held by the propagandist. (3) *Hasty generalizations* refers to consciously or subconsciously misquoting the findings of a study or misrepresenting the findings of a single study by generalizing them to a larger population than is justifiable. In other words, it involves taking a small fact and blowing it up into a large implication. (4) *Glittering generalities* involves an attempt to persuade a listener by using

---

* Although it has been noted that propaganda tends to employ more emotional than logical appeals, it should be emphasized that few arguments are either purely emotional or purely logical. In reality, most arguments include elements of both logic and emotion. Definitions of the amount of each characteristic differ, according to the perceptions of the message originator and the message receiver. It is more reasonable to view logic and emotion as two ends of a single continuum on which arguments may be placed. Viewing the logic-emotion continuum in this manner, most arguments best suited for propaganda are those which are more toward the emotional than toward the logic end of the continuum.

words, phrases, and statements which have virtuous sounds (*e.g.,* liberty, representative government, democracy, racial equality, social relevance, and so forth). Glittering generalities have high positive connotations for most people. Therefore, their inclusion in a speech often tends to make people identify strongly and positively with other elements in the message. (5) *Name calling* is self-explanatory. When President Nixon called a group of college students "bums," several students who did not perceive themselves as "bums" identified this as a name-calling device. The general use of the device is to employ nicknames which have unfavorable connotations to attack or degrade the personality of an opponent or opposing group. (6) *Labeling* is closely related to name calling. It involves making a semantic generalization about a person, object, or event on the basis of limited observation or experience. For example, the labels "Jew," "Catholic," and "Protestant," carry with them many generalized connotations. Yet we all know Catholics who don't like fish, Jews who send Christmas cards, and Protestants who smoke and drink. Propagandists who use this labeling device capitalize on the generalized, usually negative connotations labels carry with them. (7) *Transfer* is, in essence, the reverse of labeling. It attempts to associate "positive" attributes identified with one person or group with the cause expounded by the propagandist. For example, a propagandist might seek to be identified with a church group because churches have negative connotations for relatively few people. He seeks to have the positive feelings associated with the church "transferred" to his cause. (8) Similarly, *testimonials* attempt to identify the positive image of the person giving the testimony with the cause of the propaganda campaign (for example, Art Linkletter testifying as to the destructive nature of drugs on youth). Testimonials are employed most frequently in advertising and politics. (9) *Plain folks* devices are those in which speakers attempt to appear humble and part of the "in crowd" by using middle- or lower-class language, dressing conservatively (or in some cases loudly) as the occasion demands. It involves an attempt to identify strongly with the audience the speaker hopes to persuade. (10) *Dynamite words* are those which have strong emotional impact on listeners. Examples of such words are "boy" (to a black listener), "old man" (to a father), "rape," most "four-letter" words. These words tend to cause "signal reactions" in the minds of a listener, that is, reactions that are not logically derived or based

upon deliberative judgments. (11) The final device, the *bandwagon,*
is extremely common. It usually is employed very successfully by
teenagers, who use this device when coaxing their parents to let
them do what "everybody else is doing." Politicians also use this
technique with great effectiveness.

The devices noted above represent a relatively small proportion
of those used. Most of them are neither inherently good or bad. They
may be used for unworthy causes or they may be used to influence
others for laudable purposes. The importance of recognizing the
above devices lies in simply being aware that propaganda is being
transmitted. After you recognize it, you then must make a subjective
decision regarding its value.

PROPAGANDA ANALYSIS

Several of the suggestions regarding ways of handling rumors
also apply to propaganda, especially those involving the analysis
of observation versus inferences and the assessment of motives attributed to the message originator. Propaganda assessment is more
difficult than rumor analysis because the source of the message is
often unknown, and evidence cited often is not available for examination. However, the Institute for Propaganda Analysis suggests, in a very precise and clear statement, a possible plan for examining propaganda. "First, conduct a preliminary examination of
what is said . . . followed by a search for the evidence on which
such a statement may rest and the means whereby it may be veri-
fied." Next, execute a "study of the motives which may have existed
in the mind of the person making the utterances. . . ." Conclude with
"an examination of the persuasive force of the statement itself, that
is, . . . [an] evaluation of its appeals to people's interest, needs,
[and] desires. . . ." This statement describing the basic process of
propaganda analysis provides the critical listener with a basic tool
to determine whether or not propaganda is being employed, and, if
it is identified, to determine whether or not its potential effects are
positive or negative for himself or other members of society.

In conclusion, keep in mind the importance of active critical
listening in the analysis of rumors and propaganda. A critical listener
can help repress unfounded rumors and minimize the negative effects

of propaganda for himself and others. Critical listeners, hopefully, will help others learn how to treat rumors and propaganda, thus reducing the negative effect of biased communication on society.

Summary

Rumor and propaganda are two types of biased communication. Rumors may or may not be intentionally biased, whereas, propaganda is always intentionally biased. Both propaganda and rumors may be good or bad, depending on how they are used.

Allport and Postman's law of rumor suggests that "the amount of rumor in circulation will vary with the importance of the subject to the individuals concerned *times* the ambiguity of the evidence pertaining to the topic at issue."

Rumors may be classified in a variety of ways, including: (1) by speed or other temporal aspects of rumor; (2) by the subject matter with which the rumor deals; (3) by the motives underlying the rumor; (4) by the social effects of the rumor; (5) as local or widespread rumors; (6) as new rumors or old; (7) as plausible or nonplausible rumors; and (8) as rumors of long or short duration.

Rumors tend to change in three different ways as they are transmitted from person to person. They tend to show characteristics of "leveling," "sharpening," and "assimilating."

The following generalizations about rumors are derived on the basis of descriptive and experimental research: (1) if people desire information they are likely to initiate rumors; (2) the range of rumors depends on number of available receivers and the receivers' respective geographical locations; (3) if people are only moderately concerned about getting information, rumors which evolve are a product of critical deliberation; (4) when rumors are initiated through specific communication channels, interaction is critical for their distribution; (5) if listeners desire information to a great extent group excitement is generated, leading to the construction of rumors; (6) when group excitement is great, a large quantity of rumors is generated; (7) when people do not perceive a problem as vital, the process of constructing rumors slows down; (8) in an ambiguous setting, even after rumors have been tested for truthfulness, most people still tend to believe parts of the rumor; (9) the more the emotional overtones accompanying a rumor, the more likely it will be distorted when retransmitted.

Several additional generalizations may be made about rumors on the basis of case studies and observation: (1) rumors usually are temporary in nature; (2) rumors tend to run in cycles; (3) the content of most rumors deals with personal events or people; (4) immediate verification of a rumor is very difficult or impossible; (5) initiators of rumors are generally not expert regarding the subject matter of the rumor.

The first step in analyzing rumors is to identify them. The same tests used to evaluate inferences may be applied to possible rumors. In addition, several suggestions can help listeners evaluate and analyze rumors: (1) check the source; (2) check with the transmitter of the rumor; (3) determine the consequences of the rumor for yourself and others concerned; (4) try to assess what motives might have contributed to the rumor; (5) conduct systematic research to uncover evidence which will prove or disprove the critical elements in the rumor.

Several clues can help determine the presence and nature of propaganda: (1) an examination of to whom the message was addressed; (2) a determination of who will benefit most if the message advocated is accepted—the communicator or the public in general; (3) the presence of emotionally laden words or ideas.

The Institute for Propaganda Analysis has identified a variety of propaganda devices which should be guarded against by listeners. These include: (1) half truths; (2) card stacking; (3) hasty generalizations; (4) glittering generalities; (5) name calling; (6) labeling; (7) transfer; (8) testimonials; (9) plain folks; (10) dynamite words; (11) bandwagon.

The recognition of propaganda devices will help in the analysis of the intention and motives of the speaker. A systematic approach in the analysis of propaganda is necessary to assess the impact of propaganda messages on society.

QUESTIONS FOR DISCUSSION

1. *What are some examples of each of the types of rumor mentioned in this chapter (short duration, long duration, local, widespread, etc.)?*

2. *What are some examples of propaganda that may have beneficial effects?*

3. *What should be the role of the news media in controlling the transmission of rumors?*

4. *What personal motives tend to make people want to believe rumors without verifying them?*

5. *How can laymen be helped to understand the potential dangers of reacting to rumors and propaganda without taking time to verify their truthfulness?*

6. *What other forms of biased communication can you identify in addition to rumors and propaganda?*

LISTENER FEEDBACK AND RESPONSE

by Kathy J. Wahlers

Content Objectives for Chapter 7

After completing this chapter, you should be able to:

(1) Define, orally or in writing, the term "feedback."

(2) Describe, orally or in writing, the importance of feedback.

(3) Draw a model, identical to the one presented in the chapter, of the three levels of feedback.

(4) Describe and differentiate, orally or in writing, among the three levels of feedback.

(5) Describe, orally or in writing, the four classes of feedback responses.

(6) Describe and differentiate, orally or in writing, between: (a) rewarding and punishing feedback; (b) nondirective and directive feedback.

(7) Distinguish, orally or in writing, between listener control of the speaker: (a) during the speaking situation; (b) prior to the speaking situation.

(8) Describe and differentiate, orally or in writing, the problems in interpreting the feedback message arising from: (a) the participant-listener; (b) the observer-speaker.

(9) Distinguish, orally or in writing, between: (a) intentional feedback effects; (b) unintentional feedback effects.

(10) List at least seven guidelines for encoding feedback.

Imagine yourself surrounded by a shield made of soundproof one-way glass. You can see through the shield and hear sounds in the "outside world," but no one can see or hear you. The shield, in effect, prevents you from responding to the messages of others; in other words, it keeps you from giving feedback.* Since you cannot provide feedback, speakers do not repeat messages you do not understand. They also do not take advantage of knowledge you possess and, consequently, make needless mistakes. You begin to feel frustrated and aggressive. Your influence and impact on others has been reduced to zero. However, even though you may have minimal influence on the speaker, his message still may produce a change in your behavior.

As long as the shield remains intact, the influence is unidirectional from the speaker to you, the listener. When the shield is removed, your feedback can influence the speaker's communication behavior and the communication cycle is completed. Thus, when restrictions such as our make-believe shield do not exist, speakers and listeners alike modify each other's behavior through the process of message initiation and feedback.

Fortunately, listeners do not have shields around them which prevent them from responding to messages. However, many listeners create their own figurative "shields" by neglecting their responsibility to provide meaningful feedback to other communicators. The primary purpose of this chapter is to demonstrate the importance of feedback in the communication process. In addition, several levels of feedback, patterns of response, and guidelines for providing meaningful feedback are presented and discussed.

Three Levels of Feedback

Feedback is generated at three different levels, depending on the nature of a communication event. Perhaps you can best understand the distinction between the levels by applying the following example to Figure 1 on page 108. Imagine sitting in an audience and

---

* "Feedback" will be defined more precisely later in this chapter, but a working definition at this point is, "a perceived message transmitted to indicate the level of understanding and/or agreement between two or more communicators, in response to an initial message."

listening to your favorite singer. As you become excited, you may
begin to jump up and down; and as you jump up and down, you
become more excited. You may be only vaguely aware that your excitement is causing those around you to become more excited and
that their excitement is stimulating you. By observing you individually
or the audience as a whole, the performer is able to determine if his
message is being received or if some modification in the message is
necessary.

This example illustrates the three different levels within the
communication process at which feedback may exist. Through *self-
feedback* you excite yourself. *Listener-to-listener* feedback may
excite you, may cause you to excite others, or may fail to act as a
stimulus. The feedback from *listener to speaker* is likely to produce
continuance or modification in the speaker's message.

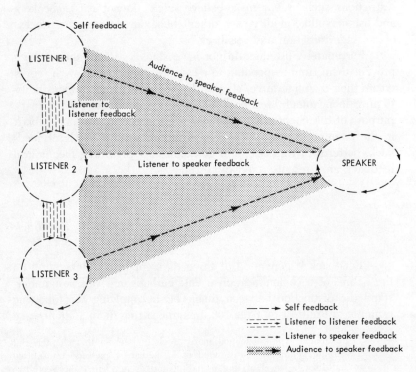

Figure 4. Levels of Feedback

SELF-FEEDBACK

You have known how to talk as long as you can remember. Consequently, if you are like most people, you probably don't think very much about the way you speak. As you communicate, your words and actions are "fed back" into your central nervous system and brain through auditory and muscular movements. Unless you stumble over a word and become sensitized to this self-feedback, the process remains at a subconscious level. Wiseman and Barker (1967, p. 27) distinguish between two types of self-feedback, external and internal.

External self-feedback is the feedback you receive when you listen to yourself. If you verbally stumble and hear yourself say "skyscaper" rather than "skyscraper," external self-feedback has occurred and can be used to help you to correct the mistake.

Internal self-feedback allows you to correct your mistakes prior to hearing yourself make them. Through cognitive deliberation as well as through bone conduction and muscular movement, you may "feel" yourself wanting to nod your head instead of shaking it for a "no" response; or, while saying one of the common tongue twisters, you may feel your tongue "twisted." Although internal self-feedback may occur in conjunction with external self-feedback, one major distinction between them is in the time of the mistake. If you realize the error before you say the word, the feedback is usually internal; if you hear yourself make the mistake and then make the correction, it probably is external self-feedback. Self-feedback is extremely useful in providing "self-reinforcement" for effective communication techniques or behaviors.

LISTENER-TO-LISTENER FEEDBACK

You may recall having seen a movie that seemed to be humorous to everyone except you. Although the movie did not seem particularly funny, you laughed along with everyone else. You may or may not have been conscious of the laughter of the other members of the group. Or, imagine an incident in which there was mob action or rioting. Afterwards, a participant reveals his initial unwillingness to participate and confesses, "I don't know why I did it, I guess I was just caught up in the spirit of the crowd."

Although this latter example may not be applicable to the majority of audience situations, it vividly emphasizes the fact that the response of any individual listener may become a stimulus which may affect the behavior of other listeners. Although you consciously may be aware of feedback from other listeners, more frequently the process is subconscious due to *perceptual discrimination*. Without such a screening process, you probably would become confused. This confusion sometimes is experienced by drug users who become highly sensitive to stimuli which ordinarily are not consciously perceived. The simple act of closing the refrigerator door may sound like the booming of a cannon.

Whether the perception of the feedback from other listeners is conscious or subconscious, certain variables tend to increase the probability that a listener will respond. One of these variables is the awareness of the feelings of the other listeners. First, an overt representation of the feeling must be present (for example, listeners are laughing). Second, the closer the proximity of the group members to each other, the more likely the listeners will be able to sense the represented feeling and react to it.*

The value a listener places on group membership is another variable which increases the probability of a listener response. The more a listener feels a part of a group, the more his membership influences his response. If a majority of group members exert pressure for conformity, those listeners with feelings of social inadequacy will be more likely to conform. †

LISTENER-TO-SPEAKER FEEDBACK

A political rally, a bull session with your friends, and an argument with your date—each communication setting maintains different norms for sending and interpreting feedback. There are four types of listener-to-speaker feedback. First is *intrapersonal feedback*, in which the speaker listens to his own message. This self-feedback was discussed previously.

Interpersonal feedback is a second type of listener-to-speaker

* See Minnick (1968, pp. 70-73).
† For further information on group pressure, see Asch (1953).

feedback. Because interaction occurs on a one-to-one basis, acceptable listener responses include verbal responses through words as well as nonverbal responses through gestures. For example, in an after-class discussion, a student may use wild gestures, contorted facial expressions, and tears, as well as words, to express his unhappiness over a grade he has received.

Group feedback may be in the form of one listener to many speakers, many listeners to one speaker, or many listeners to many speakers. When the audience applauds or is restless, the speaker receives feedback from the listeners collectively. However, the speaker also may receive feedback from each individual listener through such reactions as smiles or frowns. Group size and purpose usually determine the nature of the feedback. Feedback in a fraternity or sorority meeting frequently is limited to nonverbal communication such as facial expressions or a show of hands and an occasional verbal question or statement. This type of feedback would be out of place at a pep rally, where clapping and yelling are expected.

Mass communications feedback is the last type. Because of the nature of the mass media, such as television, less feedback between listeners and speaker occurs than in other levels of communication. An instructor teaching on educational television cannot perceive feedback from his intended listeners during transmission. He must imagine himself in the listener's place and primarily depend on self-feedback to help him correct his own message. Questionnaires or interviews may yield information for the improvement of the instruction, but generally this is not directly available or useful during the speaking situation (see analysis of nonverbal feedback).

Ordinarily, the same variables affecting the perception of the speaker's original message by the listener affect the value a speaker places on feedback. For example, feedback that is sent by a highly credible listener which expresses ideas consistent with the attitudes of the speaker will be more highly valued. Other variables affecting the value a speaker places on feedback are: learning (whether or not the speaker previously has observed similar feedback), motivation (whether or not the feedback satisfies a need, such as self-esteem), and group pressures.*

---

* For a further discussion of these variables, see Minnick (1968).

Modifying Behavior Through Feedback

When you think about behavior manipulation in the communication process, you probably think first of the speaker's control of his listener. Often overlooked is the completion of the communication cycle in which the listener controls some aspects of the speaker's behavior. Through feedback, the listener is able to exercise control over the speaker at several different points in time. Two of the most frequent points of influence are *during the speaking situation* and *prior to the speaking situation.*

DURING THE SPEAKING SITUATION

Effective communicators are careful observers of the responses of their listeners. Yawns, bored expressions, and even sleeping may suggest a lack of listener attention. Puzzled facial expressions, statements such as, "I think I understand what you are saying," tell the speaker the listener probably does not completely understand the message. By shaking his head in disagreement or—in extreme instances—by beginning a fist fight, the listener tells the speaker that he cannot accept the speaker's message.

When a listener provides feedback, he may influence or control the speaker in at least two different ways. First, he may promote a *change in speaker strategy.* This change occurs in the message itself and may cause the speaker to modify his purpose or even his topic. For example, if Dad gives an emphatic "no" to your request for ten dollars, you may decide to reduce the amount to five dollars and make the request again. Consequently, the strategy of your message has been changed as a result of your father's initial feedback.

Second, there may be a *change in the coding (verbal and/or nonverbal) of the message;* the message remains basically the same, only the symbols used to code the message are different. In addition to substituting synonyms for given words a change in coding might involve the use of different examples or evidence. To Dad's "no" to your request for the ten dollars, you may remind him of the recent yard work you completed and assure him that you will repay him soon. Thus, if Dad gives you the money, you (the speaker) are manipulating his (the listener's) behavior; but, if you change either your strategy or the coding of your message in response to your father's feedback, Dad (the listener) is manipulating your (the speaker's) behavior.

PRIOR TO THE SPEAKING SITUATION

Besides exercising control over the speaker's message during the speaking situation, the listener controls future messages which the speaker may send. Through listener behavior and perhaps even feedback to prior messages of the speaker, the listener affects the speaker's message. Manipulation of the speaker's strategy and coding of the message result from the analysis of this pre-speaking feedback, known as audience analysis.*

For example, in trying to discover the most effective way of talking his instructor out of flunking him in a course, a football player analyzed his instructor's behavior. Knowing the instructor had a keen interest in sports and in seeing the school win, the football player decided to appeal to this interest by suggesting that an F would mean his being dropped from the team. Even though he was hoping for a C, he gladly settled for a D. Although the football player manipulated his instructor's behavior to the extent that the grade was raised, the instructor controlled the football player's behavior by influencing the communication strategy and his coding of the message.

Whether sent during or prior to the speaking situation, the listener's feedback affects the behavior of the speaker. Perhaps the example of the mass media illustrates the concept most clearly; while the control the press exerts over the public generally is acknowledged, few people would deny that the press prints what its readers want to read.

Patterns of Transmitting Feedback

Earlier in this book a distinction was drawn between three types of comprehension feedback (see p. 23). One type of feedback

---

* For more information on audience analysis, see Clevenger (1966).

indicates to the speaker that you understand the message, it does not imply agreement with the message. The second type suggests that you did not understand the message, but there is no implication of disagreement. The third type of feedback is ambiguous in that the speaker is not certain whether or not you correctly understood the message. These three types of feedback are sent in each of four different classes of feedback response. The four classes of feedback response are employed in the specific response patterns described later in the chapter.

FOUR CLASSES OF FEEDBACK RESPONSE

It is obvious that people transmit feedback with their actions, vocal intonation, and facial expressions as well as with verbal language. However, many people fail to realize that silence may be a meaningful response to a speaker's message. The four classes of feedback response discussed in this section are: verbal feedback, nonverbal feedback, both verbal and nonverbal feedback, and the absence of both verbal and nonverbal feedback (silence).

Verbal feedback. Try to remember how much time you spent sending verbal feedback today. How many words did you use? Probably you would be surprised to learn the answers to these questions. People usually send more feedback each day than they realize. Verbal feedback, a form of listener response using word symbols, may take the form of either spontaneous remarks or answers to questions.

Based on content analysis,* verbal feedback may be analyzed both qualitatively and quantitatively. † In *qualitative* analysis, the speaker determines the presence or absence of a particular feedback message (what the listener did or did not say); you ask Dad for the keys to the car and he responds, "Have you washed the car yet?" *Quantitative* analysis of verbal feedback counts the frequency of the particular feedback message (*e.g.*, how many times the listener used certain word symbols); while Dad is responding to your request for the keys to the car, he mentions "washing the car" three times.

---

* Although content analysis usually focuses on speaker-initiated messages, it also may be applied to feedback responses.

† For more information on qualitative and quantitative analysis, see Holsti (1969).

Quantitative analysis may yield an indication of the intensity of feeling; when Dad mentions washing the car the fourth time, you know you will not get to use it until you wash it.

It is suggested * that you use verbal feedback:

(1) When the message is a warning or other important message and it is necessary to draw the attention of a speaker who is preoccupied with other tasks. It would be faster to yell "fire" than it would be to demonstrate the warning.

(2) When vocal inflection is important to message meanings. "I'm thrilled," said sarcastically, does not convey its usual meaning.

(3) When it is easier to say it with words. The difficulty in communicating solely with bodily action is seen in the game of charades.

(4) When visual reception is limited or unavailable, as when one is using the telephone.

(5) When it is appropriate to the situation—as in interpersonal or small group situations.

(6) When there is an organic defect in the speaker preventing the perception of visual feedback.

Nonverbal Feedback. Even as a speaker says his first words, he is receiving feedback from his listener. The speaker discerns signs of friendliness, lethargy, or hostility. Nonverbal feedback, a wordless form of listener response which may take the form of body motion or vocal intonation, provides a significant amount of all feedback occurring in face-to-face situations. For example, you nod your head, you smile or frown, you hold your hand one way to speak in class and another way to indicate "stop."

Clevenger (1966, pp. 59-64) suggests that nonverbal feedback data may be analyzed by three basic methods.

(1) *Physiological measures.* The most frequently used physiological measures are heart rate and galvanic skin response. Because the measures assess only body response, it is difficult to determine the nature of the stimulus. The feedback response may be to the speaker's message or it may be to an ant crawling on the floor. A second disadvantage is a technical one; imagine how awkward it

---

* Many of the following suggestions have been adapted from Geldard (1960).

would be to place a heart-rate monitor on each listener as well as to spontaneously analyze the data.

(2) *Audience analyzers.* One method for recording audience feedback involves the turning of a dial by each listener to register how interesting he finds the message at any one moment. Frequently, because listeners become either engrossed or bored with the message, they forget to respond or even distort their responses. There also is a difficulty in immediate quantification of the responses for use by the speaker. Although not available for general use, one development is an electronic board (much like a scoreboard used at football or basketball games) that instantaneously calculates listener response and informs the speaker of the position of his listeners. Other audience analyzers such as attitude scales or questionnaires are used primarily for audience analysis prior to the speaking situation.

(3) *Overt behavior.* This type of nonverbal feedback is the most familiar. Whether or not you wash the car is feedback in the form of overt behavior. However, you also display other nonverbal behaviors; smiling or frowning as you wash the car communicates different messages. You analyze many such nonverbal messages throughout each day, yet the process often is subconscious. While not without disadvantages (see interpreting the feedback message), nonverbal feedback seems to be most feasible and useful for day-to-day communication.

It is suggested * that you use nonverbal feedback:

(1) When encoding is difficult and it is easier to demonstrate. For example, you may find it easier to illustrate the size of a book with your hands than to verbally tell its dimensions.

(2) When emotional appeal is desired. Your compassionate grip on a friend's arm may be the best way to express, "I'm sorry."

(3) When brevity is desired. "A smile is worth a thousand words," or so the saying goes.

(4) When redundancy is needed, such as when it is necessary to encode "come on" with a hand and arm motion.

(5) When auditory reception is difficult due to unfavorable environmental problems, such as exist in mass communications.

---

* Many of the following suggestions have been adapted from Geldard (1960) and Barker and Wiseman (1966b).

(6) When there is an organic defect in the speaker preventing the perception of verbal feedback.

Both Verbal and Nonverbal Feedback. Listeners usually respond both verbally and nonverbally to a speaker's message. You probably are aware of specific occasions in which you tend to respond simultaneously with verbal and nonverbal feedback. A common example is while giving directions to the nearest gas station. You probably would point straight ahead and say, "Go two blocks down this road and turn left." However, feedback in response to a message may be verbal at one stage and nonverbal at the next. In designing an advertisement, for example, an agency first may receive verbal feedback from consumers before exposing the advertisement extensively to the public over the mass media; later, as an estimate of the advertisement's effectiveness, nonverbal feedback is received through the aggregate sales of the product.

Absence of Both Verbal and Nonverbal Feedback. As was suggested earlier, silence is often neglected as a pattern of responding to a speaker's message. More than just the absence of verbal feedback, silence also signifies a lack of nonverbal feedback. Frequently present in disagreements, silence often is interpreted as an indication of hostility. However, silence may be creative and acceptable—for example, it may communicate sympathy or concentration.

You may recall an instance when a teacher called upon a student to respond to a question and the student failed to respond either verbally or nonverbally. The teacher may have interpreted the student's silence in at least three different ways: (1) he was inattentive and did not hear the question; (2) he was trying to recall the answer; or (3) he did not know the answer. This example illustrates the risk involved in responding to a speaker's message with silence. If the speaker is not sure of the meaning of the silence, the listener has transmitted ambiguous feedback. If the speaker misinterprets the silence (e.g., if the teacher believed the pupil to be inattentive when actually he did not know the answer to the question), the listener risks a feedback communication breakdown. Because responding with an absence of both verbal and nonverbal feedback places a greater interpretive burden on the speaker, to be effective the silence should be distinct in meaning.

SPECIFIC RESPONSE PATTERNS

When a teacher suggests changing from a letter-grade system to a pass-fail system, you smile and enthusiastically exclaim, "That's a great idea!" By agreeing with the teacher's suggestion, you hope he will be more likely to implement the pass-fail system. While listening to a friend relate an incredible incident concerning his adventures the previous weekend, your facial expression communicates interest and you exclaim, "Really?" While neither agreeing or disagreeing with his story, your response induces him to explain the incident. These two examples illustrate specific response patterns. The specific patterns discussed below—rewarding or punishing feedback or nondirective or directive feedback—may employ silence, verbal, and/or nonverbal patterns of response.

Rewarding vs. Punishing Feedback.   In the context of learning theory, the act of giving feedback is a reward or punishment and may change behavior.* In this chapter, however, more than just receiving feedback, "reward" will be used to denote words or actions suggesting listener agreement with the speaker. "Punishment" will be used to denote words or actions suggesting either disagreement with the speaker or misunderstanding of the speaker's message. Thus, learning theory would postulate that knowledge of results which clearly may be either rewarding or punishing feedback may change behavior.

While learning to talk, you were given feedback from someone who repeated the word after you, praised you, or smiled at you. Although not consciously interpreting the feedback as reward, you probably continued or increased your attempts to make meaningful sounds. If, however, each time you attempted to talk, someone pinched you (that is, punished you), your attempts at producing meaningful sounds probably would have become more infrequent or even ceased completely. Whether through reward or punishment, behavior is changed.

* For a more complete review of feedback and learning, see Bilodeau and Bilodeau (1961).

The result of punishing feedback can be seen in a study by Amato and Ostermeier (1967).* Punishment, defined by the authors as disagreement, was found to have a disruptive effect on encoding; unfavorable audience feedback prompted deterioration in delivery (eye contact, nervousness, bodily movement, and fluency) for the beginning public speaker. The effect of the punishment also could be seen in the length of the speeches; the speeches receiving unfavorable audience feedback fell about one and one-half minutes below the recommended five minutes speaking time. Several explanations seem reasonable: the speakers may have forgotten their speeches or deliberately omitted part of their speeches either to overcome the audience's unfavorable reaction, or in an attempt to escape from an unpleasant situation. The important thing to remember is that punishment (disagreement) may, under some conditions, hinder encoding.

It should be noted that perceptions of reward and punishment differ from person to person. Because the meaning of feedback comes from people and not the word or action itself (see pp. 122-23), what is rewarding to one speaker may be punishing to another. In general, teachers feel that praising a student before his peers is a reward. However, praise is rewarding feedback only to those students whose peers so define it. Certain groups within our culture define teacher praise as punishment; if a teacher praises a student, often he is shunned by his peers.

To change a speaker's behavior, you may give him either rewarding or punishing feedback. However, for the reward or punishment to be effective, you must discover what is rewarding or punishing feedback *to that speaker*.

Nondirective vs. Directive Feedback. The terms "nondirective" and "directive" are borrowed from counseling theory. Similar to the client-centered approach to counseling advocated by Carl Rogers, *nondirective* feedback essentially is an attempt by the listener to replicate the message. Adapted from B. F. Skinner's theory of conditioning primarily through the use of reward, *directive* feed-

---

* It should be noted that some scholars have questioned the results of this study on methodological grounds. For example, see Combs and Miller (1968).

back involves a value judgment—the listener either rewards or punishes the speaker for his message.*

After class one day, you tell your teacher that you will be unable to turn in your term paper on time. He nods encouragingly and waits for you to explain. You begin by saying that some accidents are uncontrollable; his silence indicates that he is waiting for you to continue. You begin again by saying that because of such an uncontrollable accident, you will be unable to turn in your paper until the following week. The teacher's questioning response of "an uncontrollable accident?" induces you to describe how accidentally your little brother's artistic talent was expressed on your term paper. Through nonverbal communication, silence, and a questioning or paraphrasing of part of the message, the teacher (listener) encouraged you (speaker) to expand your message.

Verbal nondirective feedback includes a questioning repetition of the last few words spoken by the speaker and other feedback such as: "Would you explain a little more?" "Really?" "Oh?" and "I see." The tone in which verbal nondirective feedback is uttered is important; an unsympathetic tone may cause the speaker to withhold or distort information.

Similar to verbal nondirective feedback, nonverbal nondirective feedback expresses an interest in the speaker's message. Nodding while leaning toward the speaker in a relaxed, composed posture would be more encouraging than slouching in the chair and staring at a spot on the wall.

Directive feedback, because it places a value judgment on the speaker's message, is concerned with reward and punishment. After you explain to your teacher about the uncontrollable accident with your term paper, your teacher replies, "It's O.K. for you to turn in your paper next week, but I want you to understand that you will be penalized two letter grades." While initially the teacher used nondirective feedback to encourage you to explain, his later feedback was directive as he was punishing you for your message.

Since directive feedback is based heavily upon reward and

---

* It should be noted that both Roger's and Skinner's positions have been simplified in this section to the point that they represent only portions of their total contributions to counseling theory. In addition, both men have modified their positions considerably since their early writings. Consequently, the positions referred to in this section may not necessarily represent the current thinking of either Rogers or Skinner.

punishment, specific examples of verbal and nonverbal directive feedback will not be given. However, it should be emphasized that directive feedback ideally is immediate, informative, and nonthreatening to the speaker.

An effective listener does not rely totally on either nondirective or directive feedback. Keltner (1970, p. 273) notes that oversupport produces distortion and irrelevant responses as the speaker feels he should continue talking. Alternating between nondirective and directive feedback is much like driving a car on slippery pavement; as the car skids, you apply the brakes as you feel the car can take it. Similarly, you will need to alternate between nondirective and directive feedback as you determine which you need to continue the communication cycle.

Interpreting the Feedback Message

Communicating through feedback is not always easy. Usually feedback has planned effects, which are termed *intentional feedback effects*. However, misunderstanding of the feedback message may result in *unintentional feedback effects*, or feedback effects not intended by the listener. Unintentional feedback effects may occur from the incorrect sending of the feedback by the *participant-listener*, or they may result from the incorrect interpretation of the feedback by the *observer-speaker*.

PROBLEMS IN THE PARTICIPANT-LISTENER

Have you ever talked to the television or spoken to someone whom you knew could not hear you? Have you ever had your feedback fail to be perceived? These examples illustrate basic listener problems; to be effective, your feedback, first, must be observable, and second, must be observed by the speaker. A nod of the head is more encouraging to a speaker than silence, but it will be only as effective as silence if it remains unnoticed.

Occasionally, although feedback may be perceived by the speaker, it still may be ineffective and distracting to him. There are four causes of such undesirable feedback. (1) *Social conditioning.*

Although it is not socially acceptable, society usually tolerates distracting feedback such as talking or tieing a shoelace while the
speaker is communicating. (2) *Conditioning to seek attention.* Just
as some children misbehave to gain attention, some listeners give
undesirable feedback because they desire attention. (3) *Nervous tension.* Nervous tension may be released through distracting feedback
such as the tapping of a pencil on a desk or the tapping of a shoe
on the floor. (4) *Organic defect.* While not controllable by the listener, muscle paralysis, deafness, or a speech impediment make interpretation of the feedback more difficult for the speaker.

Possibly because listeners in general want to avoid hurting the
feelings of others, they occasionally mask their true feelings by intentionally sending false feedback. After listening to an ineffective
speech, you may clap because it is socially expected of you, or because you do not want to hurt the speaker's feelings, not because
you desire to reward him.

Sending feedback is a learned behavior. If you can overcome
sending feedback that is not perceivable or that is undesirable when
perceived, you can learn to become a more effective responder.

PROBLEMS IN THE OBSERVER-SPEAKER

Although the listener may send the feedback correctly, in order
for it to be useful the speaker must interpret it correctly. Whether
speaker or listener communicates, a message is interpreted in light of
prior experiences. Misunderstanding of feedback will occur to the
extent that experiences of the speaker and listener differ. If a listener
has had only pleasant experiences with the word "enthusiastic," and
the speaker thinks of overbearing door-to-door salesmen, feedback
such as, "You are an enthusiastic speaker" will not have the same
meaning for both of them. Just as the meaning of verbal language
differs between individuals, so also does the meaning of nonverbal
language; what is meaningful and acceptable nonverbal feedback
may differ from individual to individual and group to group.

In addition to the possibility of misunderstanding through word
and action meanings is the possibility of the speaker's distortion of
the feedback message. That man sees what he needs to see is evidenced in the antismoking campaign; smoker and nonsmoker alike
can find facts to support their own points of view. In an experiment

involving rewarding and punishing of the speaker's message through listener display of different colored cards, Amato and Ostermeier (1967) noted the principle of distortion; one speaker perceived many "favorable" card responses when, in fact, "unfavorable" cards were shown.

Although you can help the speaker by communicating with language having generally favorable connotations, you can never know all word meanings for all speakers. Only the speaker can overcome his own distortion of feedback, both through practice and through conscious awareness of bias in his interpretations.

Guidelines for Encoding Feedback *

Because listeners have the duty to respond to the speaker's message in order to complete the communication cycle, transmitting effective feedback should be of concern to each listener.

The following guidelines have been prepared in an attempt to help you increase the effectiveness of your feedback. They have been derived, in part, on the basis of empirical research, but primarily from communication theory and personal observations.

(1) *Send feedback that is appropriate to the speaker, message, and context.* The norms of the situation (to whom the feedback is being sent, where and for what purpose) should determine whether the feedback will be verbal, nonverbal, both verbal and nonverbal, or silence. Feedback that is appropriate at a football game probably is inappropriate in the classroom.

(2) *Be certain the speaker perceived the feedback.* If the feedback is not observable or does not gain the speaker's attention, it can have no effect on the communication cycle. Simply sending the feedback again may be inadequate in some situations. You may need to ask the speaker how he perceived your feedback and correct his misinterpretation.

(3) *Make certain the feedback is clear in meaning.* As in speaker-listener communication, secondary messages should be definite and in agreement with primary messages. Nodding should be

---

* Many of the following suggestions are adapted from Wiseman and Barker (1967, pp. 255-56) and Keltner (1970, pp. 97-99).

perceived as agreement and not sent while encoding a negative response (disagreement).

(4) *Send the feedback quickly.* A delayed response may be perceived by the speaker as ambiguous feedback. If you need a period of time to think before responding to the message, you should indicate this to the speaker.

(5) *Beware of overloading the system.* Continual nodding during the speaker's transmission may produce "noise" in the system and may cause a communication breakdown. Continual responding also may have a negative effect on interpersonal relations as the speaker may perceive the continuous feedback to be surface agreement lacking in sincerity.

(6) *Delay in performing any activity that might create an unintentional effect.* If an action is necessary and is not part of the feedback message, you should indicate that fact to the speaker.

(7) *Keep feedback to the message separate from personal evaluation.* Criticizing the speaker rather than his message may result in hostility and a breakdown in communication.

(8) *Use nondirective feedback until the speaker invites evaluation of his message.* Unless the speaker invites your evaluation of his message in a specific form of reward and punishment, employ the technique of paraphrasing his message back to him—so he realizes you understand what he is trying to say.

(9) *Be certain that you understand the message before you send directive feedback.* Rather than risking a misunderstanding by using reward or punishment in response to an incorrectly perceived message, repeat the message as you perceive it so that the speaker can correct your interpretation of the meaning.

(10) *Realize that early attempts at giving more effective feedback may seem unnatural but will improve with practice.* Just as practice by the speaker in encoding increases speaker effectiveness, practice in sending feedback increases listener effectiveness.

Summary

Feedback is important to the total communication process. There are three levels of feedback: self-feedback (both external and internal), listener-to-listener feedback (the feedback you give or receive from other listeners), and listener-to-speaker feedback (further categorized into intrapersonal, interpersonal, group, and mass communications feedback).

Both during and prior to the speaking situation, a listener is able to modify a speaker's behavior through feedback. There are various classes of feedback response and specific response patterns.

The four classes of feedback response include: verbal feedback, nonverbal feedback, both verbal and nonverbal feedback, and absence of both verbal and nonverbal feedback (silence). Verbal feedback may be analyzed qualitatively and quantitatively. Nonverbal feedback may be analyzed by physiological measures, audience analyzers, and overt behavior. In response to a message, both verbal and nonverbal feedback may be transmitted simultaneously or independently, one following the other. The meaning of silence should be clear to the speaker.

Rewarding and punishing feedback, and nondirective and directive feedback are specific response patterns. Although both reward and punishment may change behavior, the listener must discover what is rewarding or punishing to the speaker. Through paraphrasing, the listener uses nondirective feedback to encourage the speaker to expand the message without influencing its content. Through reward and punishment, directive feedback places a value judgment on the speaker's message. An effective listener alternates between sending directive and nondirective feedback to keep communication flowing smoothly.

Unintentional feedback effects may result from problems either in the participant-listener or in the observer-speaker. Several causes of undesirable feedback are: social conditioning, conditioning to seek attention, nervous tension, and organic defects. Essentially the problems in the observer-speaker arise from differences in verbal and nonverbal meanings and from message distortion.

Because feedback is important to both the listener and speaker, ten guidelines were suggested to help listeners in encoding feedback.

QUESTIONS FOR DISCUSSION

1. Does external self-feedback ever become listener-to-speaker feedback? If so, under what conditions?

2. What additional variables determine the likelihood of a listener responding to the feedback sent by other listeners?

3. In what additional ways does the listener manipulate the speaker's behavior?

4. Is nondirective feedback ever rewarding or punishing? When?

5. How does perceptual discrimination become a problem for the participant-listener? For the observer-speaker?

6. How may rewarding and punishing feedback help listeners overcome undesirable feedback?

EPILOGUE

"It seems that we shall eventually come to believe that the responsibility for effective oral communication must be equally shared by speakers and listeners. When this transpires we shall have taken a long stride toward greater economy in learning, accelerated personal growth, and significantly deepened human understanding."

Ralph G. Nichols and Leonard A. Stevens
Are you listening? (1956, pp. 221-22)

BIBLIOGRAPHY

Adams, H. Learning to be discriminating listeners. *English Journal,* January, 1947, 36, 11-15.

Allport, G. and Postman, L. *The psychology of rumor.* New York: Holt, Rinehart & Winston, Inc., 1947.

Amato, P. and Ostermeier, T. The effect of audience feedback on the beginning public speaker. *Speech Teacher,* 1967, 16, 56-60.

Andersch, E. and Staats, L. *Speech for everyday use* (Rev. ed.) New York: Holt, Rinehart & Winston, Inc., 1961. (Chapter 7, Listening, pp. 161-82.)

Anderson, I. and Fairbanks, G. Common and differential factors in reading vocabulary and hearing vocabulary. *Journal of Educational Research,* January, 1937, 30, 317-24.

Asch, S. Effects of group pressure upon the modification and distortion of judgments. In D. Cartwright and A. Zander, *Group dynamics.* Evanston, Illinois: Row, Peterson, 1953.

Barbara, D. *The art of listening.* Springfield, Illinois: Charles C Thomas, Publisher, 1958.

————. On listening—the role of the ear in psychic life. *Today's Speech,* January, 1957, 5, 12-15.

Barbe, W. and Meyers, R. Developing listening ability in children. *Elementary English,* February, 1954, 31, 82-84.

Barker, L. and Kibler, R. (Eds.). *Speech communication behavior: A selected inventory of theory and principles.* Englewood Cliffs, N.J.: Prentice-Hall, Inc., 1971. See R. Smith, Theories and models of communication processes.

Barker, L. and Wiseman, G. Applications of general semantics to nonverbal communication. *Ohio Journal of Speech and Hearing,* 1966, 2, 5-10.

————. A model of intrapersonal communication, *Journal of Communication.* September, 1966a, 16, 172-79.

Beighley, K. An experimental study of the effect of four speech variables on listener comprehension. Unpublished doctoral dissertation, Ohio State University, 1952.

Berelson, B. and Steiner, G. *Human behavior: an inventory of scientific findings.* New York: Harcourt Brace Jovanovich, Inc., 1964.

Berlo, D. and Gulley, H. Some determinants of the effect of oral communication in producing attitude change and learning. *Speech Monographs,* 1957, 24, 14-18.

Bilodeau, E. and Bilodeau, I. Motor skills learning. *Annual Review of Psychology,* 1961, 12, 243-80.

Bird, D. Are you listening? *Office Executive,* April, 1955, 30, 18-19.

————. Have you tried listening? *Journal of the American Dietetic Association,* March, 1954, 30, 225-30.

————. Teaching listening comprehension. *Journal of Communication,* November, 1953, 3, 127-30.

Blewett, T. An experiment in the measurement of listening at the college level. (Summary) *Journal of Communication,* May, 1951, I, 50-57.

Bormann, E. *Theory and research in the communicative arts.* New York: Holt, Rinehart & Winston, Inc., 1965.

Brandon, J. An experimental TV study: the relative effectiveness of presenting factual information by the lecture, interviews, and discussion methods. *Speech Monographs,* 1956, 22, 272-83.

Breiter, L. Research in listening and its importance to literature. Unpublished master's thesis, Brooklyn College, Brooklyn, New York, 1957.

Brown, C. Studies in listening comprehension. *Speech Monographs,* November, 1959, 25, 288-94.

Brown, J. and Carlsen, G. Brown-Carlsen listening comprehension test. Yonkers, New York: World Book Co., 1955. Manual of Directions, p. 18.

Brown, J. and Carlsen, G. Brown-Carlsen listening comprehension test. Manual of directions: Forms Am and Bm. New York: Harcourt Brace Jovanovich, Inc., 1955.

Bruner, J. On perceptual readiness. *Psychological Review,* 1957, 64, 123-52.

Caffrey, J. Auding. *Review of Educational Research,* April, 1955, 25, 121-38.

Carlton, R. An experimental investigation of the relationships between personal value and word intelligibility. *Speech Monographs,* 1954, 21, 142-43.

Cartier, F. Jr. The social context of listenability research. *Journal of Communication,* May, 1952, 2, 44-47.

Clevenger, T. Jr. *Audience analysis.* Indianapolis: The Bobbs-Merrill Co., Inc., 1966.

Combs, W. and Miller, G. The effect of audience feedback on the beginning public speaker—a counter view. *The Speech Teacher,* 1968, 17, 229-31.

Crawford, C. Some experimental studies of the results of college note taking. *Journal of Educational Research,* 1925, 12, 379-86.

Crawley, S. Note-taking and the use of notes. Chapter 4 in *Studying efficiently.* Englewood Cliffs, N.J.: Prentice-Hall, Inc., 1938.

Crook, F. Interrelationships among a group of language arts tests. *Journal of Educational Research,* December, 1957, 51, 305-11.

Devine, T. Listening. *Review of Educational Research,* April, 1967, 37, 152-58.

Dovring, K. *Road of propaganda: the semantics of biased communication.* New York: Philosophical Library, Inc., 1959.

Duker, S. (Ed.). *Listening bibliography* (2nd ed.). Metuchen, N.J.: Scarecrow Press, Inc., 1968.

———. *Listening: readings.* Metuchen, N.J.: Scarecrow Press, Inc., 1966.

Duker, S. and Petrie, C. Jr. What we know about listening: continuation of a controversy. *Journal of Communication,* December, 1964, 14, 245-52.

Early, M. Suggestions for teaching listening. *Journal of Education,* December, 1954, 137, 17-20.

Educational Testing Service. A brief cooperative sequential test of educational progress. Princeton, N.J.: Educational Testing Service, 1957.

Edwards, A. Political frames of reference as a factor in influencing recognition. *Journal of Abnormal Social Psychology,* 1941, 36, 34-50.

Edwards, V. *Group leader's guide to propaganda analysis* (Rev. ed.) New York: Institute for Propaganda Analysis, Inc., 1938.

Erickson, A. An analysis of several factors in an experimental study of listening at the college level. Unpublished doctoral dissertation, University of Oregon, Eugene, Oregon, 1954.

Fairbanks, G., Guttman, N. and Miron, M. Effects of time compression upon the comprehension of connected speech. *Journal of Speech and Hearing Disorders,* 1957, 22, 10-19.

Furbay, A. The influence of scattered versus compact seating on audience response. *Speech Monographs,* June, 1965, 32, 144-48.

Gauger, P. The effect of gesture and the presence or absence of the speaker on the listening comprehension of 11th and 12th grade high school pupils. Unpublished doctoral dissertation, University of Wisconsin, Madison, Wisconsin, 1951.

Geldard, F. Some neglected possibilities of communication. *Science,* 1960, 131, 1581-87.

Goldstein, H. Reading and listening comprehension at various controlled rates. Contributions to Education, No. 821. New York: Bureau of Publications, Teachers College, Columbia University, 1940.

Goodman—Malamuth II, L. An experimental study of the effects of rate of speaking upon listenability. Unpublished doctoral dissertation, University of Southern California, Los Angeles, 1956.

Green, M. An exploratory investigation of listening ability and certain factors accompanying listening in selected groups of college students in the University of Tennessee at Knoxville. Unpublished master's thesis, University of Tennessee, Knoxville, Tennessee, 1958.

Greene, E. The relative effectiveness of lecture and individual reading methods of college teaching. *Genetic Psychology Monographs,* December, 1928, 4, 457-63.

Haberland, J. A comparison of listening tests with standardized tests. *Journal of Educational Research,* April, 1959, 52, 299-302.

Haiman, F. An experimental study of the effect of ethos on public speaking. *Speech Monographs,* September, 1949, 16, 190-202.

Hall, R. An exploratory study of listening of fifth grade pupils. Unpublished doctoral dissertation, University of Southern California, Los Angeles, 1954.

Hampleman, R. Comparison of listening and reading comprehension ability of fourth and sixth grade pupils. *Elementary English,* January, 1958, 35, 49-53.

Haney, W. *Communication patterns and incidents.* Homewood, Ill.: Richard D. Irwin, Inc., 1967.

Heath, M. A study in listening: the relationships between interest educability and score in an objective examination over the factual content of an informative speech. Unpublished master's thesis, Florida State University, Tallahassee, Florida, 1951.

Heilman, A. Critical listening and the educational process. *Education,* March, 1952, 72, 481-87.

Hill, W. *Learning: a survey of psychological interpretations.* San Francisco: Chandler Publishing Co., 1963.

Holsti, O. *Content analysis for the social sciences and humanities.* Reading, Massachusetts: Addison-Wesley Publishing Co., Inc., 1969.

Horowitz, M. Listening and attitude—the interaction of cognition and affect. Paper presented to the 54th annual meeting of the Speech Association of America at Chicago, Illinois, December, 1968.

Hovland, C., Janis, I. and Kelley, H. *Communication and persuasion.* New Haven: Yale University Press, 1953.

Institute for propaganda analysis, *Propaganda Analysis,* 1938, 1 New York: Columbia University Press, 1938.

Irving, J. The psychology of wartime rumor patterns in Canada. *Bulletin of the Canadian Psychological Association,* 1943, 3, 40-44.

Irwin, C. Evaluating a training program in listening for college freshmen. *School Review,* January, 1953, 61, 25-29.

Johnson, K. The effect of classroom teaching upon listening comprehension. *The Journal of Communication,* May, 1951, 1, 57-62.

Jones, M. A critical review of literature on listening with special emphasis on theoretical bases for further research in listening. Unpublished master's thesis, North Carolina State College, Durham, North Carolina, 1956.

Kaplan, A. *The conduct of inquiry.* San Francisco: Chandler Publishing Co., 1964.

Keller, P. Major findings in listening in the past 10 years. *Journal of Communication,* March, 1969, 10, 29-38.

Keltner, J. *Interpersonal speech-communication: elements and structures.* Belmont, Calif.: Wadsworth Publishing Co., Inc., 1970.

Kerlinger, F. *Foundations of behavioral research.* New York: Holt, Rinehart & Winston, Inc., 1964.

Knower, F., Phillips, D. and Kroeppel, F. Studies in listening to informative speaking. *Journal of Abnormal and Social Psychology,* January, 1945, 40, 82-88.

Kramar, E. The relationship of the Wechsler-Bellevue and A.C.E. Intelligence Tests with performance scores in speaking and the Brown-Carlsen listening comprehension test. Unpublished doctoral dissertation, Florida State University, Tallahassee, Florida, 1955.

Kramar, E., and Lewis, T. Comparison of visual and nonvisual listening. *Journal of Communication,* November, 1951, 1, 16-20.

Krueger, D. A study of the results of teaching factors of listening comprehension to college freshmen in the basic communication course. Unpublished master's thesis, Whittier College, Whittier, California, 1950.

Larsen, R., and Feder, D. Common and differential factors in reading and hearing comprehension. *Journal of Educational Psychology,* April, 1940, 31, 241-52.

Lewis, T. and Nichols, R. *Speaking and listening: a guide to effective oral-aural communication.* Dubuque, Iowa: William C. Brown Company, Publishers, 1965.

Markgraf, B. An observational study determining the amount of time that students in the tenth and twelfth grades are expected to listen in the classroom. Unpublished master's thesis, University of Wisconsin, Madison, Wisconsin, 1957.

Matthews, J. The effect of loaded language on audience comprehension of speeches. *Speech Monographs*, 1947, 14, 176-86.

Minnick, W. *The art of persuasion* (2nd ed.). Boston: Houghton Mifflin Company, 1968.

Mullin, D. An experimental study of retention in educational television. *Speech Monographs*, March, 1957, 24, 31-38.

Nichols, R. Factors accounting for differences in comprehension of materials presented orally in the classroom. Unpublished doctoral dissertation, State University of Iowa, Iowa City, 1948.

Nichols, R. and Lewis, T. *Listening and Speaking*. Dubuque, Iowa: William C. Brown Company, Publishers, 1954, p. 13-15.

Nichols, R. and Stevens, L. *Are you listening?* New York: McGraw-Hill Book Company, Inc., 1957.

Nicholson, H. On human misunderstanding. *Atlantic Monthly*, July, 1947, 180, 113-14.

Osborn, A. *Applied imagination*. New York: Charles Scribner's Sons, 1962.

Park, J. Vocabulary and comprehension differences of sound motion pictures. *School Review*, 1945, 62, 154-62.

Paulson, S. An experimental study of spoken communications: the effects of prestige of the speaker and acknowledgment of opposing arguments on audience retention and shift of opinion. Unpublished doctoral dissertation, University of Minnesota, Minneapolis, Minnesota, 1952.

Petrie, C., Jr. An experimental evaluation of two methods for improving listening comprehension abilities. Unpublished doctoral dissertation, Purdue University, West Lafayette, Indiana, 1961.

Prince, B. A study of classroom listening effectiveness in basic communications and its relation to certain other factors. Unpublished master's thesis, University of Denver, Denver, Colorado, 1948.

Rankin, P. Listening ability. Proceedings of The Ohio State Educational Conference's Ninth Annual Session. Columbus: The Ohio State University, 1929, 172-83.

Ross, R. *Speech communication fundamentals and practice.* Englewood Cliffs, N.J.: Prentice-Hall, Inc., 1965. esp. Speech communication processes, 1-20, chapter 1.

Ruesch, J. The infantile personality: the core problem of psychosomatic medicine. *Psychosomatic Medicine,* 1948, 10, 134-44.

Schneider, W. A review of some of the literature related to listening. Unpublished master's thesis, University of Denver, Denver, Colorado, 1950.

Shibutani, Tamotsu. Improvised news: a sociological study of rumor. Indianapolis: The Bobbs-Merrill Co., Inc., 1966.

Smith, A. *Communication and culture.* New York: Holt, Rinehart & Winston, Inc., 1966.

Sorenson, H. *Psychology in education* (2nd ed.), New York: McGraw-Hill Book Company, 1948, 392.

Stephens, J. *Educational psychology.* New York: Holt, Rinehart & Winston, Inc., 1951, 313-51.

Still, D. The relationship between listening ability and high school grades. Unpublished doctoral dissertation, University of Pittsburgh, Pittsburgh, Pennsylvania, 1955.

Stromer, W. Listening and personality. *Education,* January, 1955, 75, 322-26.

————. Listening—How? *English Journal,* June, 1952, 41, 318-19.

Sullivan, G., Jr. Listening behavior in the secondary schools. *American Teacher,* December, 1946, 31, 12-13.

Taylor, S. *Listening.* In what research says to the Teacher series. Washington, D.C.: Association of Classroom Teachers of the National Education Association, 1964.

Thompson, E., Jr. An experimental investigation of the relative effectiveness of organizational structure in oral communication. Unpublished doctoral dissertation, University of Minnesota, Minneapolis, Minnesota, 1960.

Thompson, W. *Quantitative research in public address and communication.* New York: Random House, Inc., 1967. esp. Listening, 131-48.

Toussaint, I. A classified summary of listening—1950-1959. *Journal of Communication,* September, 1960, 10, 125-34.

Tucker, W. Science of listening. *19th Century,* April, 1925, 97, 548-57.

Tyler, T. English and radio today. *English Journal,* 1946, 35, 272.

Utzinger, V. An experimental study of the effects of verbal fluency upon the listener. Unpublished doctoral dissertation, University of Southern California, Los Angeles, 1952.

Vernon, M. An investigation into the intelligibility of educational broadcasts. *British Broadcasting Corporation Quarterly,* 1950, 10.

Widener, R. A preliminary study of the effects of training in listening. Unpublished master's thesis, University of Oklahoma, Norman, Oklahoma, 1950.

Wiksell, W. Problems of listening. *Quarterly Journal of Speech,* December, 1946, 32, 505-8.

Wilt, M. A study of teacher awareness of listening as a factor in elementary education. Unpublished doctoral dissertation, Pennsylvania State University, State College, Pennsylvania, 1949.

Wiseman, G. and Barker, L. *Speech—interpersonal communication.* San Francisco: Chandler Publishing Co., 1967. esp. Chapter 11, The responding communicator, 234-58.

THE
HUMAN EAR *

Introduction and Objectives for Appendix A

This brief explanation of the structure and workings of the human ear is provided for those readers who desire a deeper understanding of the physiological basis of listening—hearing. Barbara identifies and discusses the primary components of the human hearing mechanism, discusses a theory of pitch discrimination, and describes several factors which may interfere with the hearing process.

After reading the following passage, you should be able to:

(1) Identify, in writing, the three parts of the hearing organ and describe the structure of each.

(2) Describe, in a brief paragraph, the nature and functions of the Eustachian tube.

(3) Recall and recognize the names of the three small bones which occupy the cavity of the middle ear.

(4) Recall and recognize the name of the narrow, coiled tapering tube in the inner ear.

(5) Describe, in a brief paragraph, the theory most extensively held regarding the method of discriminating between sounds of different pitch.

(6) Identify and describe at least three variables which may disturb sound waves as they travel their natural course through the ear.

---

* From Dominick A. Barbara, *The Art of Listening*, 1958. Courtesy of Charles C Thomas, Publisher, Springfield, Illinois. Reprinted also by permission of the author.

. . . .

A most marvelous and complex organ of the human body is the ear. How many of you have ever wondered how one hears? Just lift up your head and listen. When a Stradivarius is well played, the sound waves pass from the violin through the air to the ear. From here on in, providing you are free of ear troubles, these sound waves are converted into electrical impulses in the auditory nerve and then relayed along the entire complicated hearing apparatus. What usually results is that we hear a beautiful blend of sounds, more delicate than any modern hi-fi can ever hope to reproduce, this because the ear has an amazing acoustic sensitivity, much finer than any instrument can approximate.

The organ of hearing consists of three parts: the outer visible

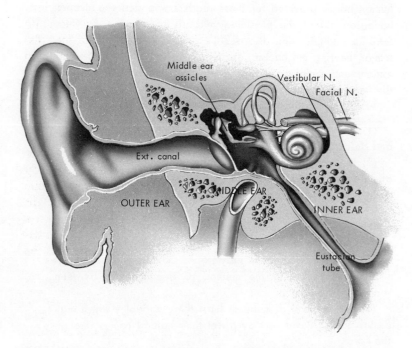

Figure 5, The Human Ear (adapted from Willard R. Zemlin "The Ear." *Speech and Hearing Science: Anatomy and Physiology.* Englewood Cliffs, N.J.: Prentice-Hall, Inc., 1968.

ear, the middle ear with its eardrum, and the inner ear. The *inner ear* is the true sense-organ. It is here that the vibrations cause the excitation of sensory cells and the initiation of the nervous impulses, whereas the outer and middle ears are structures which, in collecting and transmitting sound vibrations to the inner ear, make it possible for this complicated and delicate device to lie safely embedded in the bone of the skull. Most mammals are equipped with a natural ear-trumpet in the external ear. This is a hollow cone which can readily be turned about to face the direction from which sounds are coming, thereby making feeble sounds more distinctly audible. From this ear-trumpet a short tube leads to the eardrum or boundary separating the outer and middle ears. In man, this amplifying apparatus is poorly developed and the external ear is little more than a mere flap of no acoustic importance. The power to move or regulate it with but few exceptions is absent. Thus, although a person may distinguish sounds varying over a wide range of pitch, he is less able to discern faint sounds than a dog or a horse, and he therefore has no accurate idea of the direction from which the sounds are coming. The tube from the external ear to the eardrum is also provided with hairs and wax-secreting cells that have a filtering and protecting function similar to that of the hairs and mucus-secreting cells of the nose.

The *middle ear* is a narrow chamber filled with air and communicating with the mouth by means of a duct, known as the *Eustachian tube*. This tube is constructed in such a way that it functions like a one-way valve. Its walls are usually pressed flat together, but when the pressure in the middle ear varies too greatly from that outside, they are forced open and a little air passes one way or the other. Almost everyone has experienced the slight fullness in the ears which occurs with a change in altitude as in a fast-rising elevator or on an auto trip over mountains. These sensations are ordinarily of no importance, signifying only changes in the pressure of the air in the middle ear.

The walls of the middle ear are strong and bony except in three places. The first and largest of these is the eardrum. In the second and third, the *fenestra ovalis* and *fenestra rotunda* (oval window and round window), there are even more delicate membranes which separate the middle and inner ears. A series of three small bones which occupy the cavity of the middle ear, called the ear ossicles, are the *malleus* (hammer), the *incus* (anvil) and the *stapes* (stirrup). This last bone of the chain has its internal base in flexible contact with the fluid of the inner ear. The motion transmitted to this fluid in turn stimulates the nerve endings situated in the actual organ of hearing, the *cochlea*. Nerve currents are set up which are then carried by the auditory nerve to the brain.

Actually sound waves travel a rather circuitous route through the ear. Hearing begins with auditory stimuli passing through the air to the ear. The sound waves pass into the ear and make the eardrum, which is stretched tight like a drum skin, vibrate. This in turn transmits vibrations to the *fenestra ovalis*. This latter elaborate device is partly protective, for the *malleus* is so jointed to the *incus* that if a violent jar such as a box on the ear occurs, the two are disengaged and the shock is blocked from passing on to the more delicate inner structures. The inner ear is filled with a water fluid. The properties of sound waves moving in water are very different from those travelling in air. Now the ear bones act primarily as levers and reduce the amplitude of the vibrations, yet by at the same time concentrating the energy of the vibrating eardrum onto a window only one-twentieth its size, the sound waves become more vigorous. This is one way in which the human ear attempts to cope with the problem of transmitting sound waves from air to water.

The *inner ear* is an elaborate labyrinth of passages embedded in bone and filled with a lymph-like fluid. The only part of the inner ear concerned with hearing is a narrow, tapering tube about an inch long which is coiled into a dwindling spiral like the shell of a snail. Appropriately called the *cochlea*, this is divided into three compartments by a partition which runs along its whole length.

On this partition are situated the sensitive endings of the ear nerves. These sense cells are made up of stiff hair-like projections which are surrounded by the endings of nerve fibres. They are placed anatomically on an elastic membrane and overhung by a rigid shelf. When the fluid surrounding the apparatus vibrates, the elastic membrane bounces up and down and the sense cells are brought into collision with the rigid shelf. It is this impact with the shelf that stimulates the cells and causes them to relay impulses along the nerve fibres to the brain.

According to the authors of a most informative book, *The Science of Life*,* the following is the theory most extensively held

* H. G. Wells, J. S. Huxley, and G. P. Wells: *The Science of Life.* New York, The Literary Guild, 1934, pp. 121-122.

regarding the method of discriminating between sounds of different pitch. The diameter of the cochlea decreases steadily from end to end of the spiral much as a spiral staircase dwindles to a point at the top. Since all the structures inside must necessarily decrease in proportion, the width of the elastic membrane on which the sense cells are placed also decreases. Thus, since the period of vibration of an elastic body varies with its size, the different parts of this membrane are tuned to different notes. The apparatus in essence is like a piano or harp whose wires produce notes of higher pitch as they decrease in length. For instance, it is known that if a tuning fork is sounded near a piano when the damping pedal is down, the particular note of the tuning fork is echoed by the appropriate wire of the piano. In other words, the pulsations emitted by the tuning fork will make a wire vibrate if the wire is tuned to the same pitch.

Just so do rhythmical vibrations of the fluid in the inner ear vibrate only that particular part of the elastic membrane tuned to their own pitch. Thus we see that notes of different pitch may affect different parts of the membrane and so cause impulses to be sent to the brain along different nerve fibres. In the final analysis, it is in the brain that the sensations given by simultaneous notes of different pitch are combined to form the complex sensation of a chord.

As sound waves travel along the complicated route through the ear, there are many factors which may disturb their natural course. Any interference along this route may interfere with normal hearing. An obstruction such as wax in the ear canal changes the vibratory properties of the eardrum. Incorrect pressure in the middle ear caused by a cold, fluid or pus in the middle ear, stiffness of the joints between the ossicles as in otosclerosis, etc., all may impair hearing. Also in rare cases, the nerve endings may be unable to respond to a sound wave because of disease of the main nerve or of the brain's temporal lobe.

.   .   .   .

SOME
LISTENING GAMES,
PROJECTS,
AND EXERCISES

Below are several games, projects, and exercises which can help you better understand your own listening behavior, the listening process, and listening habits of others. In addition, several of the exercises can help you refine your listening skills through participation in simulated listening situations. Teachers may wish to assign some of these exercises in conjunction with one or more chapters in the text. Students, in classes where exercises are not assigned, may want to engage in some exercises in order to help improve their own listening behavior.

1. Prepare a report for presentation to the class which differentiates among the different types of listening behaviors needed in the following settings:

    (a) listening to classical music

    (b) listening to a baseball game on the radio

    (c) listening to a lecture on nuclear physics

    (d) listening to a "bull session"

    (e) listening to a news program on radio or television

2. Play the "control the speaker" game. This game involves manipulating the speaker's verbal and nonverbal behavior by altering the type of feedback you give him during a speech. For example, if you refuse to look at the speaker except when he speaks very loudly, you may be able to make him increase his volume until he is almost shouting. Other variations of the game include giving all

positive reinforcement to one speaker and all negative reinforcement (or punishment) to another speaker, and comparing the communication behavior of each. *Use caution and discretion when playing this game,* that is, make sure it does not cause the speaker harm when you manipulate his behavior.

3. Keep a log of the time you spend engaging in each form of verbal communication during an entire typical day. You will recall that the forms of verbal communication are reading, writing, speaking, and listening. Compare your results with those discussed in Chapter 1. Do your results confirm the importance of listening as a major form of communication?

4. Attend a classroom lecture or speech with a friend. Agree in advance that only one of you will take notes while the other simply sits and listens. After the speech, compare the amount of information retained by listening with that included in the notes taken. Was there a difference in quantity or quality of information retained?

5. Read three additional references on listening (see Bibliography). Prepare a report which synthesizes the readings, contrasting and comparing them with each other, and perhaps contrasting all three with this book.

6. Play the "listening retention" game. This game involves one person reading a passage, word by word, to a group of players. The first player must repeat the first word accurately, the second player must repeat the first plus the second word, the third player must repeat the first three words, and so forth. When everyone in the group has had a turn, the first player takes up where the last player left off. The player to successfully repeat the most words in the passage without missing a word is declared the winner.

7. Prepare a brief report on the types of listening you enjoy most. Contrast these types of listening with those you enjoy least. What reasons can you propose for your listening preferences?

8. Tape record, on two different tape recorders, newscasts delivered by different local stations or networks at the same time on the same day. Play these "back-to-back" and critically analyze differences in facts, evidence, and opinions presented. If discrepancies exist between them what factors might have caused them to differ?

9. Examine written and oral advertisements for their propaganda content. (Employ the criteria suggested in Chapter 6.)

10. Play the "rumor" game (see Chapter 6). The game is

played by having one person read a brief paragraph containing several critical facts to another person while the rest of the players (from 4 to 7) are out of the room. Then the person who heard the passage read aloud relates it to one of the people who were out of the room when it was read initially. This person relates it to another, and the process continues until everyone has heard the passage. If possible, tape record each version of the story. Then play back the entire tape and note how the versions changed from person to person. Discuss the differences and attempt to determine what "rules" for rumor distortion were in operation.

Appendix **C**

MEASUREMENT
OF LISTENING
ABILITIES

It should not be surprising to learn that there has been considerable controversy regarding the evaluation of listening ability. In the first place, as was pointed out several times in the text, scholars disagree concerning (1) definitions of listening, (2) factors which are critical to listening success and, (3) measures of listening ability which reflect most adequately the critical listening skills which people should possess.

Several scholars have constructed listening-comprehension type tests to measure retention of information. These have generally been used for specific research and instructional purposes—not for widespread use. However, a few "standardized" listening tests have been developed for general use. Two of the most widely used tests, appropriate for high school and college students, are the *Brown-Carlsen Listening Comprehension Test* (Brown and Carlsen, 1955) and the *Sequential Tests of Educational Progress* sub-test on listening (Educational Testing Service, 1957). This test is often referred to as the STEP listening test.

Both of these tests have received "mixed" reviews and reactions by communication scholars and speech teachers. Most criticisms have been focused on the validity of the tests (in other words, are they really testing listening ability, or are they testing some other trait such as intelligence, aptitude, hearing, and so forth?). Other criticisms have questioned how representative are the types of listening tested for. For example, the Brown-Carlsen listening test evaluates "aural assimilation of symbols in a face-to-face speaker-audience situation, with both oral and visual cues present" (Brown and Carlsen, 1955, p. 1). On the other hand, the STEP listening test attempts to measure interpretation and evaluation in addition to those "aural assimilation skills" (comprehension) measured by the Brown-Carlsen test. Both tests purport to test those listening skills which have been classified earlier in this text as "critical" listening skills. Other types of listening (e.g., appreciative) are not evaluated.

Even though standardized and teacher-made listening tests may be criticized justly on several fronts, it is still desirable to attempt to measure listening skills. Even though the instruments available may be relatively "crude," they are still better than none at all. It is recommended that teachers attempt to provide listening tests for students in their classes, either by employing one of the standardized tests such as Brown-Carlsen or STEP or by constructing their own test.

Some Sample Questions

Below are a few sample questions representative of the types of items which appear frequently on standardized and teacher-made tests. A review of these sample items can help you prepare to take a listening test. They also can serve as models for teachers who desire to construct their own tests.

SAMPLE ITEM NUMBER ONE

In the following sequence of numbers (read aloud by the test administrator), "8, 4, 3, 1, 3, 4," what was the second number?

SAMPLE ITEM NUMBER TWO

In the following set of directions (read aloud by the test administrator): "Turn left at the corner, go three blocks until you see the green billboard, then make a sharp right turn and it is the fourth house on the left"

(a) How many blocks were you to go after turning left at the corner?

(b) What color was the billboard?

(c) After the sharp right turn, how many houses were you to go?

SAMPLE ITEM NUMBER THREE

Given the following verse (read aloud by the test administrator): "Coeds' skirts are now so short—that watching legs is no more sport"

(a) What was the probable sex of the author?

(b) What was the central message of the verse, in your own words?

SAMPLE ITEM NUMBER FOUR *

Given the following passage (read aloud by the test administrator):

. . .

"Dr. Charles Irvin tested 1,400 Michigan State college freshmen before and after listening training. Poor to above-average listeners before training improved the most. Listening-trained students improved 9-12 percent, 9-12 percent over non-listening trained students. Listening does improve through training.

"In another study, Dr. Arthur Heilman gave students a listening test. Next, they were taught six lessons in listening. Then, they took a second listening test. Students receiving listening training improved greatly over students without training. Students with low listening scores and high IQ's improved more than other groups."

. . .

Answer the following questions concerning this passage:

(a) In Dr. Charles Irvin's study conducted at Michigan State, the greatest gain in listening ability was made by the:

---

* This passage is an excerpt from a listening comprehension test developed by Robert J. Kibler in "The Impact of Message Style and Channel in Communication," unpublished dissertation, The Ohio State University, 1962. It is reproduced here by permission of the author.

1. poor listener group
2. poor to above average listener groups
3. very poor to below-average groups
4. above-average to good listener groups
5. good listener group

(b) Dr. Charles Irvin and Dr. Arthur Heilman's studies *primarily* support the statement:

1. Listening is not closely related to hearing acuity.
2. The highest scores among a group of listeners were about six times higher than the lowest scores.
3. Listening is the most important skill that needs to be taught.
4. Listening ability can be improved through training.
5. Silence is an aural symbol.

(c) Dr. Charles Irvin and Dr. Arthur Heilman's studies compared groups with training in listening to:

1. groups with no training in listening.
2. groups with hearing problems.
3. groups competent in English literature.
4. groups of effective speakers.
5. none of the above.

INDEX